The Discovery of
Kingdom Water

ORLA
KELLY
PUBLISHING

MICHELLE KEANE

www.kingdomwater.ie
info@kingdomwater.ie

Cover design, book design and typesetting by Anú Design, Tara
(www.anu-design.ie)

Cover photography © Little Meadow Images (www.littlemeadowimages.com)

Printed and bound in Castleisland, Co.Kerry by WALSH COLOUR Print
(www.walshcolourprint.com)
Published by Orla Kelly Publishing

Kingdom Water logo designed by aidan@avalanchedesigns.ie

KINGDOM
WATER

This Book is Dedicated to The Memory of Noelle,
and to My Four Angels in Heaven

Contents

Preface

In May of 2018, a chance decision to bottle some holy water from St Michael's Well in Ballinskelligs, Co Kerry, Ireland as a gift for a friend, set me on a most strange and wonderful journey.

Over 24 extraordinary months, I saw visions granted to me by spirits and angels, met new people who helped me on my path, uncovered water with healing properties on my land, and discovered power and ability in myself I could never have imagined. At every stage, I feel I have been guided, by divine and sacred forces but also by the people – friends and family – around me.

This is a story full of strange happenings and unexplained coincidences that I see as evidence of God's love, and of the deepest workings of life that we do not always understand. Experience comes out of feeling. Heart is the door to divine.

Very quickly, I began to realise that I would need to keep a record of all that happened to me, starting with that day in Ballinskelligs. So I began to write a diary, filling it with events and visions that, at first, I could hardly believe. Life is all about the journey & the destination.

Everyone is in search of happiness, but people are seeking the right things but in the wrong places. This is why so far, to so many people, happiness comes from within,and that it can happen only upon knowing the mystery of one's own mind. In fact happiness is the most natural quest of all living beings. This is a moving tale of a spiritual guide of enlightenment and discovery through the opening of the all-powerful, the all-knowing…

This diary is what has become The Discovery of Kingdom Water.

Beginnings

I have been a person of faith for all life. I was raised in a household where there was always time for prayer, particularly the Rosary, which we as a family would say every night. Anyone who visited the house during this time took part, no matter who they were. Gratitude to God and to the Blessed Virgin was part of the everyday fabric of our lives. Even now, I cannot pass a church without going inside to light a candle and say a quiet prayer for my intentions and for those of others.

If you visit my home, you will always see lighted candles in my hall, bedroom, bathroom and living rooms. For me, these candles are a sign of God's presence, and symbols of the deep faith that I hold within. They are reminders that God is my sanctuary.

I was born and raised on a dairy farm in Knocknagoshel in Kerry, Ireland. My mother Thérèse gave birth to me and baptised me Thérèse Michelle.

I was the middle child and she called me after herself, but also after St Thérèse de Lisieux, 'The Little Flower.' She gave me a second name, Michelle, which is the French name for Michael, her father's name. He was a policeman in Rockaway, New York, back in the 1930s.

I always remember my aunt Marie telling me a story about him – that one night while on duty, he got badly beaten up and got a massive blow to his head. Later he dreamt that St Thérèse appeared to him and requested that he call one of his daughters Thérèse, after her.

She also asked him to recite a prayer to her each day of his life, which I believe he did, the Novena Rose Prayer:

> *O Little Thérèse of the Child Jesus*
> *Please pick for me a rose*
> *From the heavenly garden*
> *And send it to me*
> *As a message of love.*
>
> *O Little Flower of Jesus,*
> *Ask God to grant the favours*
> *I now place with confidence*
> *In your hands*
> *(Mention your special prayer request here)*
>
> *St. Thérèse, help me to always believe*
> *As you did, in God's great love for me*
> *So that I may imitate your 'Little Way' each day.*

St Thérèse had a short life, dying at the age of 24. Throughout her life she wanted to be accepted by the Catholic Church. After her death, the publication of her journey in the book Story Of A Soul, as well as the collection of her letters and restored versions of her journal that have continued to be published, saw public admiration for St Thérèse become so great that she was eventually canonised.

She is the patron saint of aviators, florists, illnesses and missions. St Michael on the other hand is recognised in the Bible as an archangel and has been part of Christian teachings since the earliest times. He is defender of the church and opponent of Satan, and assists in the hour of death. He is a spiritual warrior.

St Michael is patron saint of grocers, mariners, paratroopers, police officers and military personnel.

Prayer to St Michael:

"Saint Michael the Archangel, defend us in battle. Be our protection against the wickedness and snares of the devil; May God rebuke him, we humbly pray; And do thou, O Prince of the Heavenly Host, by the power of God, thrust into hell Satan and all evil spirits who wander through the world for the ruin of souls. Amen."

It's true what they say: A saint never dies, Monks, Sages and Sadhus never die.

They leave the physical body but live in the astral form.

In life, all we have is our name. And I was blessed on the 28th of September 1975 at 9.20am when my mother gave birth to me and gave me the most powerful name a child could be given.

It's ironic how my journey with Kingdom Water started at St Michael's Well, and I was called after him. This makes me feel this was my destiny, bringing me on a more incredible journey than I could ever have imagined.

The place where I was born, Knocknagoshel in County, Kerry, Ireland, derives its name from the Gaelic words 'Cnoc' or hill & 'Caiseal' which means a stone fort or oratory or a bare stone wall made without clay between the stones.

Knocknagoshel is in the northeast part of Kerry, set among rolling hills and valleys. The parish is surrounded by five other parishes – Brosna to the east, Castleisland to the south, Ballymacelligott to the southwest, Duagh to the northwest & Abbeyfeale to the north.

There are five rivers running in different directions through the parish. The chief of these rivers is the Owveg, which rises in the Lyre Mountain in the Castleisland Parish.

Knocknagoshel is 22 miles as the crow flies from the ocean. As children, the highlight of our year was the family trip to the seaside town of

Ballybunion on the Southwest coast of Ireland. That was our Costa del Sol. During the car journey, my three sisters (Norma, Myra and Delia) and brother (Maurice) would compete over who would be first to see the ocean. Arriving into the town of Ballybunion, we would see buckets, spades and windbreakers for sale, and smell the fresh smell of periwinkles and seaweed. Our first sight of the Atlantic Ocean, from the Nun's beach, always brought with it a wonderful burst of excitement linked to the water and what we would do there.

Although I never learned to swim as a child, I had no fear of water. When not at the seaside, my siblings and I, along with our first cousins, Noreen, Maurice and Geoff would swim (or splash) in the Owveg river at the bottom of our farm. I developed a great respect for water as a child and for some reason I always felt happy to be near it. I drank it, and bathed in it, and felt a connection to it.

All my life I have been drawn to water and particularly the ocean. I love the sound of the waves; the natural rhythm and flow is like a massage for my mind and spirit. I always do my best thinking when I'm by the sea.

We all know that water is essential to life. Without water, life is not possible. Our bodies are composed of on average 70% water, and we all need to consume around two litres of it a day to stay healthy. When scientists look to space and other planets, water is a significant part of what they look for. But more even than the life-sustaining properties of water is the faith that humanity has in the divinity of water, and the ways in which water can help the human journey of mind, body and soul. There are places around the world – Ganga, Lourdes, Fatima, Knock, Medjugorje and many more – where the water is believed to have healing powers, and in rivers such as the Ganga, there is even a belief that these are the homes of certain gods, and that as such, they are the guardians of life. Water so often acts as a metaphor for life and, by extension, health. It flows through the landscape, under the ground, and through the human body. The science of water and climate is and always has been evolving. It was water that made planet earth, uniquely in the solar system, it seemed a planet of change.

Here in Ireland, we have so many places with different expressions of water, many of which have specific connections to health and healing. The early Celtic cosmologists understood the healing properties of nature, particularly landscapes connected with seas, lakes, rivers and springs. They understood the way we respond to both the spiritual and physical aspects of water, and all the ways in which this can benefit us.

Twenty years ago, at a wedding, I met Keith. I remember coming home and telling my mother 'today I met the man I'm going to marry.' I just knew from that first meeting that he was my soulmate and twin flame. And indeed, we were engaged and married within a year-and-a-half.

Keith is an accountant by training and a fully accredited Qualified Financial Advisor. He has the mindset, methodology, and accountability of his training, and has been a vital support to me in all that has happened.

Keith continued to live in Dublin for the first five years of our married life, coming to Kerry at the weekends. God bless Kerry airport! At the time, I had established my own interior design brand, Mibeau Interiors, created out of my relentless passion for all things interiors.

For me, the passion began when, as an independent 16 -year-old, I was given the opportunity to design a family friend's kitchen. This modest commission kick-started my love for design, and launched a wonderful career.

My design style is underpinned by a subtle coordinated fusion of East meets West; meaning clean lines and neutral tones, blended with charming warmth and opulence. I work with homes, bars, restaurants and offices, and am honoured to be the recipient of awards including being a finalist in the Smirnoff Young Designer of the Year 1994, Trinity College.

One of the proudest points in my career – being awarded a Post Graduate Scholarship from the Scottish College of Textiles in Galashiels, also in 1994. I am passionate about making my design ethos accessible to all, and assist this by lecturing part time in Interior Design.

When I set up Mibeau Interiors, in Feb 2000, it was, from the get-go, a one-stop-shop for all interior design needs, designing and fitting out everything from a tired old sitting room, to a complete hotel project, working everywhere from Portmarnock, a coastal suburban settlement in Fingal, Ireland, to Portugal. The Mibeau Interiors brand, keeping true to its core value of high quality, simplicity and timeless elegance, has collaborated with global international brands like Ralph Lauren Home (the only online presence in Ireland), Designer Guilds, Sanderson and Harlequin, and the wider licensed product collection consists of home, accessories, fabrics, paints, wallpaper, all available to order now online at Mibeau Interiors (www.mibeauinteriors.com)

Keith and I both wanted children, but starting a family was not easy. I suffered four miscarriages, but we were blessed too, with our son, Luke, and, when I was 40, with our daughter who I christened Holly Thérèse. Both have brought untold joy into our lives. They are the reason why I do what I do, and the basis for my belief in miracles. To me, they are both miraculous, and proof that wonderful things can happen even when you have given up expecting them.

Chapter 1

A Visit to Archangel Michael's Well, Ballinskelligs, Ireland

In which I find myself embarked on a strange journey

On May 22, 2018 I had arranged to go on a boat trip to visit Skellig Michael with my friend Brid Flynn and her husband, Dean, who were home on holidays from Australia.

The day was magical from the start. We set off from the village of Portmagee, on the Iveragh peninsula of Kerry, with Paul Devane's Skellig Michael Cruises. The view from Paul's boat was just breath-taking as we looked out over the crystalline waters of the Atlantic Ocean. The walk up Skellig Michael was magnificent.

At lunch afterwards, back in Portmagee, I suggested that we go to Archangel Michael's well, in Ballinskelligs, as I wanted to bring back holy water from the well for my dear friend Tahnee, who lives in Dublin.

Ballinskelligs, officially Baile an Sceilg, is an area in the south-west of the Iveragh peninsula in County Kerry, Ireland, within the Gaeltacht in the magnificent Skellig Ring between Dingle, Waterville and Valentia Island, forms part of what is known as the Dingle Diamond.

A year previously, I had read a lovely book called The Discovery Of The Dingle Diamond which tells of a quest into the first stirrings of the human spirit, and of one simple myth – the drawing of a line on the landscape, a ley line, bringing order to some of the ancient sites. This area boasts some of the most spectacular scenery in Ireland, with its rugged coastline, scattered islands, vast mountains and miles of golden beaches with turquoise waters.

The spiritual connection with St Michael is very strong in this area. Skellig Michael, a deeply sacred place, is at a conjunction between two very important ley lines, both of which connect with sites of great spirituality, many named after St Michael, including St Michael's Mount, Mont St Michael and St Michael's Well. These ley lines also connect with the Michael line that passes through Glastonbury Tor and Stonehenge in the UK, and the main line can be traced all the way back to Egypt.

Even those who do not believe in ley lines often find they feel a strong connecting force in these places. For those that do, the fact that these sacred spots have been built over different centuries but along connecting lines, is compelling evidence of power and energies that we don't understand.

After lunch we headed off to find St Michael's Well. We went to the pier in Ballinskelligs and asked four local people we met along the way for directions. Not one of them could tell us where it was. In fact, a couple had never heard of the well.

At one stage my friend Brid piped up from the back of the car to ask if I was sure such a well even existed. I replied that I was 100% certain, and that I could feel it in my gut that it was very near.

Around we drove, through the tiny, picturesque village of Ballinskelligs, until I saw an old lady in a doorway. We stopped and asked her, and finally found someone who knew of the well and was able to provide directions. We parked and walked, up a laneway, through an estate of holiday houses, across little stepping stones over a ditch, down over a field and through a gate into the field with St Michaels Well.

Standing there with the view of the Atlantic ocean to one side and the mountains to the other, all three of us remarked that this was just heaven. I had brought two bottles with me, and filled them from the well.

Looking down into the well, I realised this holy water was flowing into the Atlantic ocean. When I turned around after filling the two bottles, I saw the figure 7 painted in white on a big stone on the ground. Somehow, over the past few months, it had felt as though the number 7 was everywhere I looked. I said to my friend Brid that I wanted to sit and pray for a while.

I sat on a rock I prayed for all the people in my life. While there, I saw a vision of St Patrick. At first I thought I was seeing things. Then the vision became clearer and stronger. It felt very surreal.

Ireland of course also has a strong connection to St Patrick. St Patrick and his followers were free to spread their faith throughout Ireland and did so to great effect. He drove paganism, symbolised by the snake, from the lands of Eireann.

Patrick was tempted by the Devil whilst on a pilgrimage at Croagh Patrick. For his refusal to be tempted, God rewarded him with a wish. Patrick asked that the Irish be spared the horror of Judgement Day and that he himself be allowed to judge his flock.

Thus, the legend that Ireland will disappear under a sea of water seven years before the final judgement, was born.

Patrick died on March 17th in the year 461 at the age of 76. His influence is still felt to this day as Nations the world over commemorate him on March 17th of every year. St. Patrick's Breastplate, is a popular prayer attributed to one of Ireland's most beloved patron saints.

St. Patrick's Breastplate

Christ with me,
Christ before me,
Christ behind me,
Christ in me,
Christ beneath me,
Christ above me,
Christ on my right,
Christ on my left,
Christ when I lie down,
Christ when I sit down,
Christ when I arise,
Christ in the heart of every man who thinks of me,
Christ in the mouth of everyone who speaks of me,
Christ in every eye that sees me,
Christ in every ear that hears me.

Deep inside my gut, I had a feeling then that something strange was taking place inside me. I felt strongly that I had been here before, and that I would be back to visit this sacred ground again. In life I have always trusted my gut, and the energy of that place felt like an electric current through my whole body. Part of me did not want to leave but after a while, maybe half an hour, I had to head back up the field with Brid and Dean.

We talked all the way about how beautiful a place this was, and how spiritual, but little did I know that this visit to Archangel Michael's Well would change my life forever, bringing me on a journey that I feel I was always meant to be on. The discovery of Kingdom Water.

Chapter 2

A Message From The Ancestors

Tahnee is a designer who creates beautiful bespoke tiaras and headgear, as well as cashmere scarves and spiritual jewelry. She is also a clairvoyant; she can communicate with those who have passed on and with spirits from other worlds.

I first met Tahnee at my friend Denise's dinner party. From the first moment, it was as if we had known each other all our lives. A month after my trip to Skellig Michael and St Michael's Well, Tahnee and her young son, Scott, who is the same age as my Luke, decided to come to Kerry for a few days holiday.

The first evening, the two of us sat in the sitting room and Tahnee said, "Michelle, your ancestors are here. They have a message for you and want me to channel them to you."

I knew that she meant what she said – I could feel a sort of divine shiver go right through my body. So I said "who's there" and Tahnee replied "your grandmother Mary Bridget, your Aunty Brid, your grandmother Nora." Then she said "there's also a man and he's egging the ladies on to make sure and tell you that he's here with them." I asked Tahnee what his name was, to which she said, "They're showing me a picture of a rally car, and saying he's 72 years old. They're also showing me a chair upholstered in leather that is worn thin on the arms."

At first I told her I knew no 72-year-old man, but when she mentioned the chair I suddenly remembered my father's uncle, Joseph Thompson, who used to call to our house and sit in a chair he had made himself, upholstered in leather.

My ancestors spoke to Tahnee then, and told her that I would write a best-selling book and that there would be a movie made of it. They also felt that I would go into politics within a few years, and said they would support me in this. They said beautiful things about my son Luke and daughter Holly. They asked Tahnee to tell me to pray for them as they can see how hard I'm working and want to help me.

They also requested, through Tahnee, that I put a plant in the corner of the sitting room to remind me of them, and to take good care of the plant. I listened and agreed to all they said.

Then Tahnee said to me that she felt strongly the presence of Our Lady in the house, and a powerful energy from all around her.

The next day I gave the bottle of Archangel Michael well water to Tahnee and told her where it came from.

That night, after the children were in bed, Tahnee, Keith and I sat in the kitchen having a cup of tea when I felt a powerful shiver run right up through my whole body, sent, I felt, by the Archangel Michael. I knew something strange was happening and wondered aloud, "what is going on?"

Then Tahnee said to me that the angels were showing her a natural spring of water, coming from a ditch on our land, and telling her that there are seven more such springs. She said "they are showing me a 3 and a 4, and telling me that whatever is in this water is going to heal people all around the world." The angels told her that there was nitrogen in the water and other important minerals that have healing properties. They also told her to ask me if I have any questions for them. I did of course, so Tahnee said "take off your necklace and we will use that as a pendulum." I took off the necklace and asked her to ask Archangel Michael were there indeed healing properties in the water. Immediately the pendulum began to move in a clockwise circle, to indicate 'Yes.' Then I asked 'do they want me to test the water?' and again the pendulum indicated 'Yes.'

My husband was speechless watching this. I could feel in my gut the power of what was happening.

We could not go to bed. Not after that. Instead, Tahnee and I walked my property at 2am in our dressing gowns. She said, "this is a very spiritual ground and the angels are telling me that they want the word 'Heaven' to be used in some format in the naming of the water." I looked up at the night sky and it was so beautiful; that vast space with its borderless flow of clarity stretching on out to infinity. There was smattering of low level flat clouds spread out to the horizon. I went to bed then but could not sleep after all that had happened. It was as if I heard a voice inside me say 'you must test the water tomorrow.' I prayed to God for direction and also to thank Him for what Tahnee said. As I prayed, I felt a deep peace and understanding, and at last I went to sleep.

I am an early bird, so despite the late night I got up and walked around my property at dawn, to feel the energy of the place. This has always felt like a spiritual place to me, but for some reason, that morning, I felt it more strongly than ever before.

I drove to my local town of Castleisland and bought five sterilised bottles and sterile gloves. When I arrived home with the bottles, I went up the stairs and woke Tahnee: "wake up Miss, we have water to test." Off we went, the two of us, with our sterile gloves, and took samples from the spring on our ditch.

It bubbles up over the ground so is easy to reach, unlike the seven underground springs.

We drove to Southern Scientific in Farranfore, an Irish, family-owned environmental consultancy and testing laboratory, where water samples can be comprehensively tested.

There we met scientist Michael Murphy, a chemical consultant who specialises in analytical science and environmental science who is also chairman of Southern Scientific. He agreed to run a full mineral chemical analysis test on the water, and said it would be three weeks before we would have the results.

On the way back in the car, as we laughed and chatted, Tahnee said " Michelle, could you get your hands on a set of divining rods? We need to find out where the seven underground springs are." I considered who in the locality might have such a thing, and then remembered my dad's first cousin, Tom Thompson. Tom is the son of Joseph Thompson, the man who contacted me through Tahnee. Tom used to divine and I knew he would have divining rods so we headed up to Thompson's farm and met Tom's lovely wife Eileen. She said that Tom had not used the rods in over 15 years and had no clue where they were, but that a neighbour of theirs, Richard Murphy, could divine.

That evening, Richard called to us with the rods. First, Tahnee divined for the seven springs and found each one of them. Then we asked Richard to divine also and he confirmed that we would have no bother digging a well in any part of our site. Tahnee gave my husband Keith the rods and he too was able to divine.

Then Tahnee said I should have a go. At first I refused but she insisted that I had the gift for divining so I took the rods and immediately felt them move in my hand, but I said to her "I cannot," and handed them back. I was thinking to myself, between being a wife, a mother, and running a very busy interior design business, the last thing I need is another string to my bow!

Three weeks passed and Tahnee had gone back to Dublin when finally, on a Friday evening at 6pm I got the full scope of the water analysis emailed to me from Southern Scientific. The results showed that there were over 25 minerals in the water, with evidence of 17 Rare Earth Elements.

I sat and looked over these results for an hour. I could not believe the minerals found in our water. I showed the results to Keith and like me he was speechless. I called Tahnee in Dublin and said, "I have the results back and there are over 25 minerals and evidence of 17 Rare Earth Elements, including ytterbium, in the water."

Tahnee was speechless. There was silence, and then she said "the angels & your grandmother Mary Bridget are talking to me now and they are delighted that you tested the water. They have a very strong message for you, Michelle. They want you to open up one of the seven springs and test that water too." She also said the angels were telling her that the following six months would be crucial, that it would be a rollercoaster, and not at all easy for me to get people to believe in this but, she said, "they say have given you this gift as they know that you have the business acumen, the energy and determination to bring this water to everyone in the world so they can reap the benefits of this healing water."

That night, Keith and I did not sleep a wink. The two of us had our iPads out, researching all the minerals mentioned in the report. Every mineral on the list, when we looked it up, had unexpected benefits. For example, strontium is a trace element also found in seawater, it regulates bone formation and helps the body to absorb other minerals more efficiently. Some minerals even had healing benefits for cancer. One particular element that really stood for both Keith and I was boron, which is often taken by people in supplement form, and is believed to affect the way the body handles other minerals such as calcium, magnesium, and phosphorus. It may also have antioxidant effects. Usually, boron is found in the sea and in land close to the sea – we were 22 miles away, which made it an unusual find.

And it was not just beneficial to bodily health. Ytterbium, for example, is used in certain steels and its metal could be used to help improve the grain refinement, strength, and other mechanical properties of stainless steel. We also found europium, widely used as a red phosphor in television sets and as an activator for ytterbium based phosphors.

We spent the whole weekend researching all the various minerals, and on Monday morning I rang Michael at Southern Scientific and asked him what he made of the report. He said he was baffled himself, and advised that we get the water tested again as we would need to prove that the presence of these elements was consistent. He also said that he had never come across some of the elements before, and knew very little about all their health benefits. He suggested we get a biochemist to fully analyze the results and go through all the individual minerals and elements.

I agreed with Michael that another full scope test on the water was a good idea, and provided him with new samples. These results took two weeks, and once again the rare earth elements showed up – but this time only 4 out of the original 17.

I rang Michael and said, "where did the other 13 disappear to?" He said he did not know what to think, but insisted that we do another test again in two weeks' time.

My gut kept telling me that those Rare Earth Elements were still there, that they could not just disappear from the ground. Keith was as puzzled as I was. I rang Tahnee and told her what was happening, and she said "the angels & your Grandmother Mary Bridget are telling me that you're right; that those Rare Earth Elements are still in the groundwater."

At that stage, Keith and I decided that the only way we would know for sure would be to open up one of the seven springs and test the water. We decided to investigate the cost and the process of opening up one of the springs.

Chapter 3

The Spirit of Water

Having decided to investigate the process of opening one of the 7 springs, I felt I had to research why I was so drawn to water in the first place. I wanted to spend time learning both the physical and emotional health benefits of water. I also wanted to understand the scientific reasons why being near water sets my mind and body at ease. I needed answers that would reveal how we think about these questions, and the remarkable truth about the benefits of being on, in, under or simply near, or indeed drinking, a glass of water.

The human body is about 70% water. The brain is said to be almost 75% water and is very sensitive to dehydration or depletion of its water content. The human body and the cosmos itself is essentially made of five elements:

Earth (bones and muscles)
Water (blood)
Air (breath)
Fire (heat)
Space (the emptiness within)

If any one element is taken out, the body will collapse. Of all the five elements, water is the most important – with an imbalance of water, many ailments including sinusitis, asthma, swellings, blood thinning or clotting, problems of urination or diseases of the reproductive organs occur.

While the majority of the earth's surface is covered by oceans, these oceans make up just a small fraction of the mass of the planet. Earth is the only planet known to have bodies of liquid water on its surface. The temperature, along with an ample amount of atmospheric pressure within the zone allows water to remain liquid for long periods of time. However, evidence also points to water on other planets in our solar system. In 2012, NASA confirmed the liquid water flows intermittently on present day Mars, however liquid water on Mars wouldn't necessarily be the same as liquid water on earth. If our solar system tells us anything, it is that our universe is drenched in water. Quite literally, there is water everywhere. Maybe, just maybe, that's a hint that we might not be alone as we think.

The moon controls the tides and rules over the biological rhythms of plant, animal and human life. Her monthly cycle is the archetype of all life cycles. As the mother figure in astrology, the moon governs the menstrual cycle, breasts, stomach and childbirth. For the modern western mind, the subject of the moon influencing reproductive lives can sound esoteric or outlandish, but there is ample ancient lore, anecdotal evidence and scientific studies that seem to prove that fertility, water and the moon are connected in mysterious ways.

The five elements of the five fingers are dispositions of the vital force, the *Pran Shakti*. Maximum energy flows to the tips of these fingers but these five fingers represent different components of *Pran Shakti*:

Thumb- Fire (*Agni*)
Index finger- Air (*Vayu*)
middle finger- Space (*Akash*)
Ring finger- Earth (*Prithvi*)
Little finger- Water (*Jal*)

Just like water, people must be allowed to flow freely as the principle of nature is that people are mostly water. The consciousness of our ancestors is passed down from one generation to the next – through blood, it's the water that circulates throughout our bodies. Water carries within your thoughts, prayers, actions, no matter where in the world you are.

As the seasons change, so does the atmosphere, and what is it that gives life to this planet only water?

Water is the fertiliser for all the natural beauty in the world. Without water clouds would not form, flowers would not grow, meadows would not be green, rainbows would not exist. The deeper the ocean, the deeper water goes.

Without water nothing lives. It is the main source of energy – the 'cash flow' of the body. Water generates electrical and magnetic energy inside each and every cell of the body. It provides the power to sustain life. Water prevents DNA damage. It energises food. Water gives life and shine to the eyes. When water reaches a cell, it brings the cell oxygen and takes the waste gases to the lungs for disposal. Water helps reduce stress, anxiety, depression. Drinking a glass of water separates the sensations of hunger and thirst. If you want to lose weight, water is a way to achieve that. Drinking water helps us sleep better and reduces fatigue. As we grow older, water can help reduce the risk of Motor Neurone Disease, Parkinson's and Alzheimer's. It integrates mind and body functions and the ability to realise goals and purposes.

Water is the main lubricant in joint spaces and helps prevent back pain. It also dilutes the blood and prevents it from clotting during circulation.

The beautiful thing about water is that it is the most powerful medication in the world. It needs no doctor's prescription. It is freely available and is the medication your body needs when stressed. Nothing substitutes for water. Coffee, tea, juice – these are not the same as water. Water should be drunk first thing in the morning to correct dehydration produced by sleep, and before exercise to promote sweat. Anytime you feel thirsty, you should drink a glass of water. If you feel constipated, drink three glasses in the morning.

Every 24 hours, the body recycles the equivalent of 40,000 glasses of water to maintain its normal physiological functions. Water should be drunk in eight 250ml portions throughout the day; topping up in the same way that you wouldn't let your car run out of petrol.

When God created the universe, he chose water as one of the seven planets. Pressures in the ocean are almost imaginably great. They are the reason that the depths of the ocean remain nearly as hostile and unfamiliar a place as the surface of the moon. Just 10 metres of water provides the equivalent of an entire atmosphere's worth of pressure. The pressure at two kilometres below sea level is two hundred times greater than the atmosphere at sea level. This pressure is also great the reason that it took so long for the discipline of oceanography to catch up with what any individual sailor knows in the gut: that water moves quickly and in ways that are somehow both ordered and chaotic.

Today many of us have chosen to ignore God and look only to science to help heal the world. We lose sight of the real meaning of life by becoming too dependent on modern technology so that we miss the warning signs God sends us. He created the universe and gave us the gift of water, and everything else, from the herbs growing wild in our ditches. He gave us the ingredients to survive and live happy, healthy lives, but unfortunately we humans are slowly destroying the wonders of the universe.

Our ancestors instinctively knew the infinite power that water possesses. Water if the life force – from the ritual of a new-born's first bath, to a dying person's final sip. The fact that water plays a significant role in Christian baptism, and the religious role played by water from the Ganges in India, illustrate its sacred energy.

We humans on this planet need to wake up and acknowledge and explore the potential of water. That way humankind will be saved and each one of us will become happier and stronger and more content. Water teaches us something greater than ourselves. Until we begin to respect that we are all children of God, we will never understand the true meaning of water.

Masuru Emoto was a japanese author who said that human consciousness has an effect on the molecular structure of water. Emoto said that water was a " Blueprint for our reality" and that the emotional "energies" and "vibrations" could change the physical structure of water. Emoto's water crystal experiments consisted of exposing water in glasses to different words, pictures, or music and then the freezing and examining the aesthetic properties of the resulting crystals with microscopic photography. Emoto's book "The Hidden Messages in Water" was published in 2004 was a New York Times bestseller.

I often think of my discovery with Kingdom water, he is one man that I would have loved to share this experience with, as he totally understands water like no other, but sadly he passed away on October 17,2014. I feel his spirit is walking right next to me on my journey discovering Kingdom Water.

Humans started exploring the planet, and have always followed water. Crossing oceans gave way to new discoveries. The immeasurable sense of peace that we feel around water gives us a chance to escape the hyper-connected, over-stimulated state of modern life, in favour of a rare moment of solitude.

Our love of water is pervasive and is the reason why we go abroad. The need to be by the water can be hard to articulate – the feeling is so powerful it can't be easily described, but we each know that we need it, like it, and are willing to pay to experience it. Without water, we miss a part of ourselves.

I felt I needed to open one of the seven springs and have the water tested, and conduct my own research. I wanted to discover how Kingdom Water could develop into a natural mineral water and become the basis for something strong and wholesome. I needed to learn and research all the minerals within the water and find out what each of them does. I was going to take the plunge and carry out my own investigations and get this water onto a commercial footing, just like my ancestors wanted, but first, I felt we needed to go back to the basics.

We need to listen to the sounds of water – the whoosh of the ocean, the drip of gentle rain. We need to feel water against our skin. We need to take long looks at the ocean and rivers and waterfalls that surround us. We need to bless ourselves with water. We need to thank God for letting us shower in water. Let this sacred journey of discovery of Kingdom Water help us in our efforts to understand the health benefits of water, but also to respect water just as our ancestors did.

Chapter 4

Old Friends
and New Acquaintances

I receive an offer of help

Wednesday the 10th September, 2018 the sun was shining. I was in my studio, working. I could hear the faint chirping of birds, and golden rays of sunshine lit up the garden around me. I had been in my studio since 5am. Being a creature of habit, I did what I always do at 10.30am – I downed tools for 10 minutes to enjoy a good strong mug of coffee.

I was sitting outside, sipping my coffee, when my friend Denise, pulled up in her cream-coloured convertible VW Beetle. Denise is someone who will fill your day with happiness. She is everyone's friend and problem-solver, the partner of my father's old school friend Johnny Byrne from Duagh, a neighbouring parish, and the person who first introduced me to Tahnee.

That morning, Denise and I sat chatting over coffee, and a voice in my head told me to tell her about the water. So I did. I told her about Tahnee's visit, about what my ancestors & the angels had said, and all about the testing of the water.

Denise's eyes opened wide. She was speechless for almost five minutes. I value Denise's advice, so I asked her if she thought we were mad. She paused for a moment and then said, "Michelle, this is huge. The fact that the angels and your ancestors have told Tahnee to pass on this message to you – you have to open up one of the springs and see what's there."

That day, over lunch, Denise said, "I will give you the €20,000 to get the water out of the ground." I nearly choked on the chowder I was eating. I was speechless. I said, "are you crazy? We're getting way ahead of ourselves here."

Denise said, "Michelle, this is so powerful. You have to go for it or you will be regretting it all your life." We spent a long time talking, and I wavered between 'will I, won't I…?' I wondered what Keith would think, and questioned myself, but Denise was adamant that she wanted to do this, and deep inside my gut, I knew this was right. Eventually, I accepted her incredibly generous offer, and told her I would pay it back.

When I told Keith about Denise's offer, his first response was to say he did not know if I should accept. We talked for a long time, and I told Keith that without his blessing I would not go ahead, but that I felt I could trust my gut, and that the worst thing that could happen is that we would have our own supply of water.

Keith listened carefully, and accepted what I had to say. He was amazed at Denise and her generosity, but also in her confidence in me and my ability to pull this water out of the ground against all odds.

The following day I rang Morgan Lenihan from Lenihan's Well Drilling in Glin, County Limerick, Ireland. He said he would call up to look at the spot where we wanted to drill and discuss our options.

That night I asked Keith to divine all seven springs again, and to feel which one of them was the most powerful. There was one in particular where he felt the energy of the rods most strongly.

I videoed him and sent the videos to Denise, who identified the same spring that Keith and I had, but also said "get Tahnee's advice on which one to open." I did, without telling her anything, and Tahnee picked the same spring that we had chosen. I like to see those coincidences as signs of God's love, and reminders of his constant presence.

Tahnee also said, "ring a guy I know called Jack. He's the best diviner in Ireland and he'll tell you the exact spot for the well." I phoned Jack at the number Tahnee had given me, and told him my story. Jack said, "I am in a situation here at the moment but I will buzz you back in a few hours. I promise you that I will ring you back."

I was delighted when I put down the phone, but I could feel my energy changing. I felt tired, so tired that I said to Keith, "I know it is only lunchtime but I have to go to bed as I am exhausted." I slept solidly for five hours. I got up for an hour then but had to go back to bed again. I will never forget the tiredness that overcame my whole body. And I kept thinking 'why hasn't Jack phoned back?'

I woke on Sunday morning, still tired. I wondered, 'how can I still be so tired? This is weird.' At 10am Jack called and asked how I felt. I said I was exhausted and had had to go to bed. He started laughing and said, "that is ok." He said from the moment I had spoken to him yesterday, he had been working on my energy.

Jack told me my life would never be the same again. That could have frightened me, except I had begun to understand the truth of it already. My life had changed; I knew that.

Jack said he would be down the next day to divine the well, and that he would bring his friend, Dennis. I said, "Ok, but what will he do?" To which Jack responded "you have to trust me that Dennis will help you with the water." When you first meet Jack, you cannot but feel his kindness, his presence, but most of all his spirituality. As a diviner, Jack connects what lies beneath the surface with what is above. He has been divining water springs and sources in Ireland all his life. He is a deeply spiritual man and also channels advice from angels, spirits and ancestors.

Dennis is a gifted psychic medium who heals and guides people, trying to make the sick healthy and give hope to those who feel failure. He inspires people to succeed and to lead pure spiritual lives.

Having these two gifted men in my sitting room was a surreal moment for me, and I immediately felt a strong soul connection with both of them. Dennis began talking to me in a very frank and matter of fact manner, saying that St. Martin's presence was there with us in the room and that it was a very strong presence. He also said that St. Germaine had a strong presence in the room. He told me that I had a connection with St. Martin, to which I laughed and told him that long ago in primary school I used to sell the St. Martin magazine.

Then Dennis told me many things that astonished me. He began by saying:

"I had a dream eight months ago, that I would be calling to a girl in Co, Kerry about healing water, and when I drove through the gates to your home, and saw your face, that dream came flooding back to me. Be assured, this was all meant to be."

Dennis told me to get copies of the following books, Soul Mates and Twin Flames by Elizabeth Clare Prophet, and Karma and Reincarnation by Barbara H Martin and Dimitri Moraitis; that these books would help me understand and change my life.

Then Dennis asked me if I had noticed a lot of white feathers inside and outside my house over the past eight months, to which I replied that I had. He said, "A lady passed away here and those feathers are a sign from her that she is so happy that this water has been gifted to you."

He asked me to stay focused on him and look him straight in the eye. He said, "who in your life made you conform to everything? Look at your house, look at your note taking, everything's perfect." I told him there was a teacher who used to physically abuse me in school, and the perfectionism came from that. Dennis said, "that inner child fear is still with you."

He told me that my husband, Keith, was a monk and a rich scholar in his past life, that he over-thinks issues and is an excellent time-keeper; the total opposite to me – the Ying to my Yang in fact.

He told me that there were rich minerals in the ground and that the water must be bottled at source. He told me that only I have the power to bless this water. He said that my mother was gifted and her mother was also gifted, and that I had inherited it from them both, and from my father too.

I knew already about my father's uncle, Jim Thompson, who was renowned all over Ireland for his cures. People would come from everywhere to his home in Headley's Bridge, Knocknagoshel.

His cures – made from herbs and water – were so successful that even 25 years after his death, they still came looking for him. I knew he had passed his healing hands on to my father, Luke Keane, and now Jack was telling me they had come to me.

Around that time, Keith came home from Castleisland and joined us. Dennis greeted him and told Keith that he is a healer with gifted hands, and a logical thinker.

When Dennis finally finished with me, I thanked him and tried to absorb all he had said. Then he turned to Jack and said "she is all yours now." Jack was sitting around the table, listening, and now he looked at me for maybe three full minutes without saying a word.

When he finally spoke, he said, "Michelle, what are you thinking?"

I replied that I was wondering what he was going to tell me. He asked me how did I felt since I contacted him on Saturday. I said, "I feel a change, a nice change. But I have felt wrecked and tired too."

He said that was ok and that he was working on my energy, that there was a lot of work to do. He said, "You have to stop questioning why this has happened to you and just accept that this is your journey. This is your destiny and that it's going to be a beautiful journey for you as a family." He told me to look into his eyes, which I did. Then he asked me to show him a picture of my father's father, which I also did, and then he said, "I have to go to a quiet room and I'm not to be disturbed. I will come out only when I'm ready."

I escorted him to our bedroom where there is a nice comfy chair while Dennis went outside to walk the perimeter of our property.

After over half an hour, Jack came back and said, "I'm ready to start divining for Kingdom Water."

Chapter 5

Divining Talbots Stream

In which the first sacred spring is found

Jack explained that the first thing we needed to do was clear the water lines in my home.

He told me that two brothers in military uniform had once owned the land and, both knowing how valuable the water was, one brother had killed the other for it. He could see men wearing red coats, as if they were in the army, in the 1800s, and saw that the place had gone to ruin after the famine. He told me that the very spot where I had put him to sit in my bedroom was where the brother was killed.

Jack went on to say that earlier again there had been a river running through this place, and in the middle of it a big black rock, where those who had done evil deeds would be left, tied up, for months at a time. He said that many had died there, and because they had horrible deaths, the energy of the springs never left the land. All this energy had to be cleared and released.

Jack explained that on the Saturday when we first spoke, he purposely told me that he would call me back in a couple of hours. He said that he had immediately begun to work on my energy, and did not call me back because he found my energy to be at such a high voltage that he had to stabilise it. He said he could hear me saying 'why isn't Jack calling?' but that he had to ignore that. He told me again that I had strong spiritual gifts.

Then he began dowsing the kitchen, hallway, sitting room and our bedroom.

When Jack reached our bedroom, he asked me to sit on the bed and hold out my left hand. He pulled a glass pendulum from his pocket and said the names 'Darcy' and 'Keane,' which are mine and Keith's surnames, and then "I ask that the spirits leave this property and clean the lines." I must have held my hand out for three or four minutes, but nothing happened. Jack asked me if I was afraid, to which I replied no. He asked me if I wanted him to remove the spirits and I told him I did. Then the pendulum began to swing for 'yes.' Jack repeated this exercise with Keith, and within a few seconds the pendulum began to swing again for 'yes'. Jack left the room for a few minutes and when he came back, he said "Michelle, what happened here was very powerful and has never happened to me before, that someone has gone against me." There had been a spirit working against him, but he dispelled it.

Jack explained to Keith and myself how divining with rods works. He taught us how to respect the rods, and said that while Keith had done the divining until then, he felt I would be better because of the strength of my spirituality.

He said the healing properties in the water would help fertility in women, and he was adamant that the destiny of the water was in my hands.

We went outside to dowse the land. Jack said to me "I'm looking for a stream with the source of the water, and I need you to give it a name."

I replied instantly that it needed to be called Talbot's Stream as my address is Talbot's Bridge and my gut said to call it Talbot's Stream.

Jack began divining and asked the land to show him the source of Talbot's Stream. He followed the line of the source and divined the exact spot in which to bore the first well of the seven springs at exactly 4.15pm that October afternoon. The place where Jack divined was in the middle of my tarmac driveway.

I circled the spot on the tarmac with gold spray paint. While I did this, the same strange shiver went through me that I first felt in the kitchen with Tahnee back in July when we spoke of the Archangel Michael. I knew this was another powerful sign from the angels and I said a quiet prayer of thanks to the angels, to Our Lord and Our Lady, and for Jack and Tahnee.

Fifteen minutes later, Jack divined the second of the seven springs

He gave me strict instructions to tell the driller that he was not to make a mess of my well. He told me that we would hit water at 100 ft. and then I would have to make a call on this. With that Jack gave me the rods to keep.

I thanked Dennis and Jack for coming and told them to call again if they were ever passing. Jack shook my hand and said, "you will see me faster than you think." As they drove off into the sunset, I could feel a huge vibration running through my body. And the feeling of anticipation, of excitement: something we experience as completely natural and spontaneous was about to happen, yet destined to happen. The great mystery of this Kingdom Water was that sense of destiny.

I realised in that moment that the angels, my ancestors and spirit guides were by my side, and that God had gifted me this water.

Chapter 6

First of the Seven Springs

In which I open the first spring

The day after Jack and Dennis's visit, I heard a voice in my head telling me to go back to Archangel Michael's well in Ballinskelligs, to pray for help and guidance in opening the first of the seven springs. So I drove back to Ballinskelligs and bought three bottles to fill with water from the holy well.

I continued down the fields to the well and I went to fill the first bottle. But the well would not allow me. I asked Archangel Michael if I could take the water, and he let me fill the bottles. I had brought a leaf from the angel garden I had planted at the back of my house the year before, before any of these things had yet happened, and I left it there on top of the well.

As I closed the gate of the field behind me, a sick feeling came over me. I stopped half way up the field and asked Archangel Michael did he want me to put back the water or could I keep going. My instinct told me to keep going and the sick feeling left my body.

The following day I visited Archangel Michael's well in Lixnaw, in North County Kerry, Ireland, a deeply sacred place. I prayed and filled a bottle of water from the well. By the time I got home, I had to shower straight away because I was sweating like mad. I felt a warm sensation all through my body, like a healing heat.

On Tuesday 9th October, 2018 Morgan Lenihan called to our house to discuss the spot where Jack had divined. I told him Jack said we would hit water at 100 ft. and that if we did not we would have to stop, and that he was not to mess up my well. Morgan gave a hearty laugh and promised that he would not. We shook hands on the deal and he agreed that he would come the following week to bore the well.

The following day my brother Maurice called down to dig a trench in the garden so that we could lay a pipe to carry the water from the well, once drilled, into the house. Maurice told me I was mad to dig for a well in the middle of my yard, rooting up half the garden and breaking concrete. I told him that I wanted the best drinking water, that I had taken advice from the best water diviner in the country and that is where it was divined.

Maurice's response was "if you think the water there is any different to the water anywhere else on the property, you must be living on a different planet!"

I found it very hard to keep a straight face and at one stage had to go into my office to laugh without being seen. I knew he had my best interests at heart however, and sure enough he said, "I'll dig where you want but I still think you are crazy."

The day of the digging came, and from the moment I woke, I knew the day would be special. The countryside stretched before me like a great quilt of golden, brown and green squares held together by the thick green stitching of the hedgerows. I felt that never in my life had I been so in control of a situation.

At half-past one Morgan drove his drilling machine onto the spot where Jack had divined. My father had called down to the house and I brought out a chair for him to sit on. I had Keith on standby to video everything that happened. I texted Denise and Tahnee a photo, and Tahnee texted back to say the angels were bouncing everywhere. I shook some of the holy water from Archangel Michael's Ballinskelligs well and said a silent prayer that all would be well.

Morgan cranked up the machine and began to drill. I felt a warm feeling go through my whole body, and a complete calmness. I looked over in the direction of my father and I could see he was praying with his rosary beads that I would find water. I knew that this was very powerful, because at that stage I had not told any of my family what exactly I was doing, only that I was drilling a well.

I stood and watched Morgan drilling and at 93 ft. we hit water. The flow was poor and I told Morgan to keep going till he hit 100 ft. and then stop. At 100ft he stopped, but the flow was still weak.

I told Morgan that I need half an hour to think over my options – should we stop, as Jack had said, or keep going in hope of a greater flow of water? I rang Jack but there was no answer. Then I rang Tahnee and she said, "you need to call this yourself. Whatever decision you make will be the right one."

After 20 minutes I said to Morgan "keep going." I felt that he would hit a good flow of water at 124 ft. At 123 ft. he hit such a flow that the water shot high up in the air, like oil does when you see it struck in the movies. That was a surreal moment – to see water sprouting up into the air – and I felt a miracle was taking place right before my eyes. I cried then, to think this water had been down there under the earth for over 600 years.

Morgan said then that if we kept going, to a depth of 160 ft, we would hit a river – he could gauge this by the power and flow of the water. I turned to my father and asked him what he thought. His reply was that he was saying the Rosary all the time that we would get water. A miracle for sure, he said.

So Morgan kept drilling and sure enough, when we got to 160 ft he said, "we've hit a river." His advice was to keep drilling for a further 20 ft or so, to create a sump (a pit in which liquid collects), which we did, finally finishing at 180 ft.

Morgan left and I could not get over the sense of calmness, satisfaction and achievement that I felt. When we are at peace, we are engaged with life and safe, protected from stress, our immune system grows stronger and we become more resilient. Our outlook brightens and we see more opportunities. I felt then a sense of something transcendent, something eternal. Call it God, a spirit, or by no name at all. Something strange was happening; I knew it.

That night I called Jack Curtin, known locally in Knocknagoshel as the 'Water Doctor' to order a submersible pump. I told him I needed to get a sample of the water out of the well to test it. He said he would be on in the morning to me.

Keith, who had videotaped the whole drilling process, covered the well so nothing could get in. I again blessed the well with some of Archangel Michael's water and said a thank-you prayer to God for sending me this gift.

That night I rang Jack to tell him about the day's events. He was over the moon at the way things had worked out for me. He said, "everything is going according to Gods' plan. Just stay grounded. Move on to the next step and get the water tested."

I also rang Tahnee and she said, "do you realise what you have done? You have pulled water out of the ground that has been there for hundreds of years. The angels are so happy for you."

Then I called Denise, and she too was beyond ecstatic for me. I always know that Denise will bring me back to reality, and sure enough she said, 'so what's the next stage?' I told her it was to test the water and she said "do it straightaway. There's no stopping you now."

Keith and I sat down that night in the sitting room with a glass of wine in front of a roaring fire, to celebrate what we had both achieved. We both slept sound that night after a job well done.

The following morning, Jack Curtin, the Water Doctor, arrived. He got the pump installed and brought a water pump up from almost 200 ft. underground. I had an empty glass and I said "Jack, fill it up." That morning, I drank the first glass of Kingdom Water. As I sipped the water, I knew it was special. I felt an electric current run down the inside of my body. The vibration and energy of the water, and the smooth rich taste of minerals, were remarkable. Jack remarked how clear the water looked.

Keith drank a glass of it then, as did Jack, and they both agreed that this was beautiful water.

I told Jack to leave the pump on all night as Keith was taking a sample in the morning, back to Southern Scientific for testing. By then, Michael from Southern Scientific had purchased a new plasma mass spectrometer. He said it would allow us to look for more elements and to see them at lower concentrations – something that would give us more information about the water source.

I had to go to Cork the next day as I had been invited by Enterprise Ireland to speak on International Women's Enterprise Day, on how to help women in business take their ideas to a global level. I arrived at the reception of the hotel, and found a white feather on the ground as I walked in. As I was waiting to check in, another white feather fell from the handbag of the lady in front of me. While on stage as part of a panel discussion, in front of around 180 people, people started tweeting 'what's the story with the white halo on stage around Michelle Keane?' I did not realise that there was any white halo around me until I was shown photos afterwards.

When I look back on that day in Cork, I see that there were greater forces at work. Sometimes you have to look for these coincidences in life, and other times they are so obvious that you can only laugh and thank God and the angels. These gifts of white feathers and the aura around me are simple proof that God is present and that my loved ones and their spirits surround me, lift my heart and give me the strength to keep going.

Chapter 7

Seeing Visions

In which the angels send me a telepathic message

On Saturday 20th October, 2018 Keith went to Waterford with the kids for the weekend, to visit his mother. I had a back-log of work to catch up on, so I woke at 5am and bounced out of bed. I'm a real morning person. I love the early part of the day and feel you can do a day's work between 5am and 8am with no distractions and only the sound of the dawn chorus as the birds begin their daily ritual of chirping in the new day.

There I was, all alone in the house. First, I decided to polish the floors as they would get a chance to dry while the kids were away. It was still pitch dark outside, so I had the kitchen lights on. I was hoovering the floor when a light began to flash. At first I thought I must have hit the table lamp switch by accident, but then I remembered that it's on timer and so I could not have turned it on. I started hoovering again, and then I noticed the same light flashing on and off.

I stood up straight and looked up. It was one of the four recess lights that was flashing. Looking at it, a shiver went down my spine and I felt something very strange. I actually felt almost afraid then, and turned the lights off so the flashing stopped. Even then, I felt that something peculiar was happening around me. I finished polishing the floor and went out to my studio to work.

At 10.30am, I took my morning break as usual, with a mug of strong coffee and something told me to phone Jack. I told him what happened earlier and he asked me how I felt at the time. I told him I got a fright, but maybe it was just that the bulb needed changing. Although, I said, the lights are LED and I only got them last year and the life span is usually seven years. At that, Jack said, "right, just take time to sit in the kitchen for 10 minutes and try to feel and listen to what is happening."

I said I would but the day was busy and I did not get a chance until much later. I went out to dinner that evening with a friend, and I came home, at about 7 o'clock, I put on the fire in the sitting room, lit all the candles and made myself a coffee. I love watching X Factor on a Saturday night, so I turned on the TV. Then I thought of what Jack had said earlier, about sitting down to feel and listen, so I paused the TV, and just sat quietly at the kitchen table.

I was not there for more than two minutes when the recess light began to flash on and off. This time, I could actually hear the light switch being turned on, whereupon the light would flash on, and then be turned off again. I counted 14 seconds between each flash.

I got out my phone and took a video of what was happening. I wanted something to show Keith and Jack, in case they thought I was going mad and making this up.

Sitting quietly on my chair, I noticed an aura underneath each of the four recess lights, dropping down to about two inches below the light. The aura was blue, and like a beam in that it moved, beaming up and then down. After about a minute, a black circle, about two inches in diameter, began moving across the ceiling from the recess light that had been the first to flash. The black circle moved across the ceiling, stopping at a point just over my head, and then moved back again into the light. The light flashed on, and the black circle moved out again.

It did this several times, beaming back and forth across the ceiling from the recessed light to the point above my head, getting bigger each time. Then, inside the circle, appeared a picture of an old lady's face, with a very old-fashioned hairstyle. The picture was familiar but I could not place it. It appeared three times, then went away. Another, smaller black circle appeared over my head and this showed me the moon three times. It too disappeared, and yet another circle appeared, this one with a picture of a fiery-red diamond in it. This all lasted about 10 minutes and the light was still flickering on and off, almost an hour since I had first turned it on.

I walked over to stand under the recess light, whereupon it changed colour to a bright yellow and then a deep shade of blue, and finally a shade of pink. With that, the three other recess lights also turned the same shade of pink. I had never seen anything like it. Never even heard of any such thing happening. Frankly, I was terrified. The lights continued to flicker, on and off.

I tried to call Keith but he was at a birthday party and so I could not tell him what was happening. I rang Jack then, and I told him. He said he was in the middle of a job and that it would be two hours before he could call me back. I said "Jack I'm terrified. Should I be going up to my mother's, to stay there tonight?" He said "No. Go back into the kitchen and turn off that light and turn on any other light you like and simply continue about your business." I said I was scared and he told me to relax, that I was in the safest house in Ireland tonight.

That calmed me down. I decided to do what he said. I turned off the recess lights, decided to pour myself a nice glass of red wine and continue watching the X Factor. As I was sitting there on my sofa in front of a roaring fire, I noticed the picture of my grandmother, Mary Bridget, on the sitting wall. It was the same face as I had been shown on the kitchen ceiling.

Jack phoned me back two hours later, just as he promised, and tried to explain what was happening. He said, "the angels are sending you telepathic messages. Since you opened the well, a portal of water spirits has been released, along with the water that was underground."

To that I said, "Jack, are you mad? What the hell are water spirits, portals and telepathic messages from angels?" I was totally confused. Jack told me that I had to stay very grounded, that this was very powerful and was all part of my journey with the water. He told me that my life would never be the same again, and that there was no going back. All I could think was, 'what the hell is happening to me?' I had not asked for any of this, and if I am totally honest, I was actually pretty frightened by what was happening.

Jack said that in time I would be able to listen to and understand the telepathic messages that the angels would send me again. I asked him what he meant and he told me that, of everything I had been shown in those black circles on the ceiling, the moon was the most important sign, because the moon governs the tides of water.

He said that the picture of my grandmother, Mary Bridget, was a symbol that she had given me this gift. The picture of the fire-red diamond was a sign that the angels and water spirits were saying this is very rare and precious. Jack totally calmed me down, as only he could. Even so, I said "I will not sleep a wink tonight." To which he said "you will sleep sound; you're in the safest house in Ireland." Jack was right. I went to bed then, and fell into the deepest sleep I have ever experienced.

The following night Keith came back from Waterford with the kids. When they were in bed, I showed him the video and then he said he would sit in the kitchen with me and see if anything happened again. Sure enough, Keith heard the light switch go on and off, and saw the recess light flashing. A beam of light appeared, with blue on either side, and I saw three statues of Our Lady in the beam, but they were very small. Then a picture of a woman's head with hair coiled in an unusual style, like a Greek goddess, appeared on the opposite side of the ceiling to the flashing light. I said "Keith, can you see that picture of a Greek head?" and he said, "no I cannot see a thing." Pictures of rocks appeared three times. These pictures were much larger than the previous night, nearly a foot in diameter, and crystal clear. I kept saying "Keith did you see the picture of the rocks?" and he kept saying, "no, all I can see is the recess light flashing on and off."

The picture of my grandmother Mary Bridget appeared again, three times and the lights turned pink. This time, unlike the night before, there was a triangle in the light. Meanwhile, a second recess light began to beam the same pictures to a different point on the ceiling.

A small moon appeared over my head and stopped there for a few seconds. Again I said, "Keith did you see the moon." He said, "I see nothing." The moon was shown three times, and then the outside of the recess lights turned blue in colour. After that, I had to stop looking because I had such a pain in my neck from staring at the ceiling.

Keith and I went into the sitting room and I said, "do you believe me?" He said, "I do, but it's hard for me to comprehend as all I heard was the light switch turning on and off, and all I saw was the recess light flashing." I knew he was doubting me – and I could not blame him, external doubt feeds self-doubt; the number one dream killers and sometimes, even your dearest ones cannot see in you what you can see for yourself. Sharing your vision and getting others to stand behind you is not always easy, and I was not about to underestimate the task in hand, just as my ancestors had said getting people to believe me would be a roller coaster of a ride. But I knew it would all work out as I had the blessing of my ancestors behind me and that was all the affirmation I needed. I figured the Angels would look after the rest for me.

I rang Jack again, and told him everything and asked why Keith could not see what I saw. He said, "these telepathic messages are for your eyes only." He said again that I needed to keep myself grounded and say nothing to anyone else yet, as people would think I was mad. The following night I looked at the lights for about 20 minutes and nothing happened. I talked to Keith about it and he said, "I would prefer if you did not do that again." I could see he was worried about me.

On Wednesday 24th October at 8pm, Michael from Southern Scientific phoned me as I was on my way home from work, with the results of the third water test. He said that the results showed that there were indeed Rare Earth Elements ("REE") in the water sample and many minerals, almost 45 in all, and that he had never come across a mixture of water like this sample.

One REE was europium – which has never been found in any water in Ireland before – and another was ytterbium, as well as chromium, titanium, cobalt, copper, selenium and mercury. Michael's advice was that there was such a diversity of elements in the water that I really needed to pinpoint them, and their function, and I would need the expertise of a biochemist.

Michael believed the water could be of benefit as a pharmaceutical product, and said that I would need to treat this carefully as a project, but that it could be very fruitful. He said if I could prove the use and health benefits of these elements, pharmaceutical companies would be beating down the door to buy it.

I rang Denise and Tahnee, and they were both ecstatic. I spoke to Jack too. He and Dennis were on their way to India, but he said that as soon as they were back, they would call to see Keith and me. He also asked "how many more signs do you need?", and how I would feel if I had to move out of our family home. Even as he said it, I knew that ever since Tahnee's visit, I had been gearing myself up for that possibility.

I got home and told Keith what Michael had found in the water. Keith began researching REE on his iPad. When I looked over, I saw a picture that caused me to shout to him to stop and save what he had found. It was the exact picture – the rocks – that the angels and water spirits had been showing me in the orbs. It was ytterbium.

About three nights later, I sat on my own in the sitting room watching TV. The recess lights were on, and again the beams began moving across the ceiling. They showed me many different pictures of rocks, the moon, the fire-red diamond. I thought, how strange that now they are in the sitting room, not just the kitchen. I tried to take photos but I could not. They would not allow me. The pictures came out black. I think that was a message from the angels and water spirits that this was meant for my eyes only.

The following Sunday, Keith went into town and while he was gone, I was reading the paper when I looked up to find five orbs spinning on the ceiling above my head. I stood up and walked underneath them, and jumped. The more I jumped, the faster they spun. They were still there when Keith came home from two, so I asked him "can you see this?" He said he could. I was so happy that finally he could see them, because he would not worry that I was mad any more.

The orbs drew a cape on the ceiling. I researched the spiritual meaning of cape, and from there on I looked up the meaning of every image they showed me. They repeatedly showed a rock which looked like a head of cauliflower, which I now know represents the REE strontium, an alkaline earth metal that helps to increase calcium absorption and boost bone formation.

At last, the pictures and images shown to me were beginning to make sense. Gradually, I was beginning to understand that there was far more than I yet knew to this water and the portal we had opened by drilling the well.

Chapter 8

Winter Solstice

In which I meet new friends, and hear much of interest

Around the middle of December, Jack and Dennis arranged for me and my family to visit a kinesiologist, Patricia Quinn, who lives in Tallaght. Kinesiology is the scientific study of body movement, and addresses physiological, biomechanical, and psychological dynamic principles and mechanisms of movement.

In addition to this, Patricia, who specialises in working with children, is a nutritionist who teaches how to achieve and maintain optimum health by following a balanced and nutritious diet. And how, by altering our eating habits, we can relieve conditions such as insomnia, stress, headaches and loss of energy. She has written several books, including Healing With Nutritional Therapy and Beating Candida Albicans.

We drove to Dublin and stayed that night at the Jurys Inn Christchurch, where we were unexpectedly upgraded to the penthouse suite. That night, I woke up from a deep sleep to find the angels and water spirits were present. Using the same method as before, they showed me a large windmill pictured on the ceiling, and the figure 7 on the wall. This went on for an hour while everyone else was sound asleep. I looked up the spiritual meaning of windmill and read that a windmill harnesses the wind and is also designed to harness spiritual energy, much as a boat does with its sails. Thus a windmill, symbolically, is like a person with a vast amount of spiritual energy being put into them.

Then I looked up the spiritual meaning of the number seven and found that the Angel number seven is a wonderful and important message to receive, because it means support and encouragement. It suggests that Divine support is on the way, and is an assurance that whatever you are planning or thinking of, will be the best thing for you, and that your angels are supportive of these plans. They know that you are capable of making the best decision and so they send the number seven to reassure you, so that you will not start doubting yourself or your decisions. After reading that, I went back to sleep feeling very content.

We were due at Patricia Quinn's house for 12 noon on the 21st December, the winter solstice. I brought Patricia some of the Archangel Michael well water from Ballinskelligs, and a bottle of my own Kingdom Water.

On first meeting Patricia, one cannot but feel blessed by the warmth of her welcome. For a small lady she has a mighty presence, with an infectious smile. She has an air of grace about her that makes her look like an angel. Jack describes Patricia as a walking encyclopaedia and that exactly sums her up. She has been healing people, adults and children, all her life.

That meeting with Patricia was extraordinary. First, she healed Keith through the permission of my body and said that he had the most wonderful life energy, which he certainly does. She prescribed various vitamins and fish oils, and recommended that he take a rest for 20 minutes every day.

Then Patricia said that we as a family needed a tree of life healing from Jack and Dennis. This is a special healing, coming from the tree which symbolises immortality, that is carried out for a fresh start, to create positive energy, good health and a very bright future.

Patricia told me that I needed to tell Jack about my four miscarriages, and said she felt that I needed a baptism and burial for each of these miscarriages. It was hard hearing these things spoken about, but I trusted Patricia, and felt that she was right in what she said.

The kids went off for a drive then with Keith, and I spent the next few hours on my own with Patricia in her kitchen chatting. I told her the whole story of my journey with Kingdom Water. She said, "this is going to be a worldwide cure and that it will heal people all over the world. Michelle, there are many books in this journey."

She also said that my story reminded her of the story of Lourdes and Bernadette Soubirous, and that such a thing only happens when there is a connection to the Virgin Mary. Patricia said she had never met an energy like mine, commenting that after five hours together I did not seem tired at all, that the healing of Keith had not knocked a stir out of me, and that I was running my office from her kitchen table. I asked why she had chosen the Winter Solstice day for me to come to her to discuss my water and she said I did not choose it, Jack had chosen the day. I thanked her and wished her a fabulous Christmas.

That night, we met Jack for a meal before we left Dublin. He was delighted with the way the day went with Patricia and said he knew that we would forge an instant connection. He agreed to do the family tree of life healing for us after Christmas, as Patricia had suggested.

The following day, while conducting my research into water, I came across an article in the business section of the Sunday Independent on Oscar Wilde Water, the CEO John Hegarty and his marketing director Rory McLoughney. I found the article very interesting and felt, reading it, that I had a connection with John Hegarty's passion for water. I cut out the article and filed it away with all my other research.

Sometime later, I heard that Constance Harris, fashion editor of the Sunday Independent had spoken to Tahnee about her great friend John Hegarty, who owned Oscar Wilde Water.

Constance said I should get in contact with him, as he would give me good advice about the water. The name immediately rang a bell, and I remembered the article I had kept.

So I rang John, and explained who I was and what I had found. He was so encouraging and said he would love to meet me and Keith. I agreed to visit his bottling plant in Borrisoleigh, Co. Tipperary, Ireland to talk to him and get his opinion on Kingdom Water.

Keith and I drove to meet him and I brought my chemical analysis certificate with me along with a sample of Kingdom water. John, it turned out, was a walking encyclopaedia on water. He knows everything to do with water, how to test it, bottle it, market it and is a serial entrepreneur.

John tasted the water and felt it was rich in minerals. He said "you should get it tested again with another laboratory, just to compare the results, and he recommended a place in Prague in Czech Republic where a full battery of tests would be carried out.

John gave us a full tour of his bottling plant, which he had bought from the old Tipperary Water Company. It was a very impressive set up, fully automated under 15,000 sq. ft. of warehousing. He showed us the location of their well, and the rods that were used to divine the first well for Tipperary water. For some reason I had brought the divining rods that Jack had given to us, and John asked me to divine his place. I divined the spot where my energy felt the strongest.

By the end of the day, I felt that Kingdom Water and John Hegarty had a big connection. John was fantastic, he listened to and encouraged me, and has become a rock of support in guiding me on my journey with Kingdom Water. When we got the water test results back from Prague, they were practically identical to the certificate of analysis results from Southern Scientific.

We had the most magical Christmas day that year. Both Keith and I agreed that it was the best ever. Then, on the 27th December, my children were together playing in my bedroom and I was videoing them. Through the lens of the video camera, I saw many orbs flying across the room. Later, I played back the video to Keith and we counted about 20 flying around while the kids played, unaware.

Two days later, in the sitting room during the evening, Keith and I both noticed that the angels were again showing us a picture of a cape or cloak. I looked up the spiritual meaning of cloak for a second time, and explained to Keith that capes and cloaks help connect us with higher powers and spirits, and help us to build connections with the universe and God. A cape or cloak can also increase our intuition and connect with certain energies.

I was so happy that Keith was now seeing these symbols as I was. I spoke to Jack and sent him the video of the kids playing on my bed, and the cloak. He said, "Michelle you have to sit alone in the sitting room and ask the angels and spirits not to let your children see these signs." As a mother your natural instinct is to fiercely protect and guard your children from any harm and I knew that I had to honour their innocence and joy in their life, so I did as exactly as Jack requested.

Chapter 9

New Year, New Beginnings, New Messages

In which I face doubt

Tuesday, January 12th 2019. The sky had darkened to a faint violet colour on a rainy winter evening. Keith came in from work and reminded me that I was due to go to Castleisland to give blood, something I do regularly, because blood is needed to save lives. I always feel good after I do this.

That evening, while lying on the stretcher in the Community Centre main hall, where the mobile blood clinic sets up, I looked up at the ceiling, which is nearly 40 ft. high and watched as an angel, nearly 8ft high, appeared to me in a bright red colour. By now I knew that this colour represented the angels offering me wisdom. Once again, the orbs appeared and showed me pictures of rocks.

I could not reach for my phone to take a video as I was hooked up to the machine, giving blood, but the sight of these large orbs, moving around at speed, was just unbelievable. I looked around the busy hall and nobody else had noticed a thing. That was surreal.

The nurse unhooked me from the machine once I was finished looked at me and said, "you're very pale, you look like you've seen a ghost. Are you ok?" I smiled and said, "I actually have seen a ghost. Or something," and she just laughed.

In the car on the way home I rang Jack and asked, "have many other people had this experience?" He said, "very few have your gift, so just accept it and stay calm."

Two more weeks passed and by now the angels and spirit guides were permanent visitors to our house. Every night they would send more telepathic messages.

They showed a huge circle with an egg inside it on my bedroom ceiling. That vision came every night for a week and even Keith could see it. I researched what it meant. On the whole, anything that shows an egg means fertility and creation. I kept thinking of what Jack had said on the first day the well was opened – that this water would heal fertility.

Another vision shown to me was the Archangel Michael, with a unicorn, a lighthouse, a dolphin, and a whale. I researched the spiritual meanings of all these, and found that a dolphin is peace and harmony; their animal nature balances with a higher intelligence. A unicorn is one of a kind and accepts itself for who it is. A lighthouse is a grounded structure that guides people to safety, illuminates the darkest of times, bringing love and hope.

A whale is as deep as the water in which it swims, it offers the gift of understanding, communication, family, and appreciating the beauty of community. The one comparison I could draw from them is that they are all related to water.

Jack told me that my third eye was wide open by then, and that I have the gift of clairvoyance – a gift from God that brings the ability to gain information about an object, person, location or physical event through extra-sensory perception.

The images changed as the days and weeks went on. One morning I woke up and the angels and drew a picture of a man. His outline was in blue and his face was dark. He had on a white tunic and seemed very spiritual, but with a look that he meant business. He did not look like anyone I knew and I could not understand what the vision meant. The following morning, I was shown another vision of a second man's face and shoulders. He had a lovely soft look about him and his eyes were beautiful. But again I had no clue who this man was.

I asked Jack and all he said was "one day it will all start to make sense. It's all part of the journey." During this time, I was still trying to find a biochemist to interpret the water results. I contacted Trinity College but they were unable to recommend anyone. Similar results followed with UCD, University of Limerick, and Queen's University Belfast. That was a frustrating time, and I thought then how right Tahnee was when she said the angels told her that it would be a rollercoaster of a ride for me.

Everywhere I went looking for a biochemist, I was shot down, and I began to realise that scientists do not think outside the box. No one seemed able to understand that I didn't want to be told what was in the water – I had that – I wanted to understand how the different elements interacted with each other. For example, if you had strontium and iron in the water, what would the two mixed together result in, on the principle of the whole being greater than the sum of the parts? I could not find any biochemist to answer those questions.

I spoke to Keith about the difficulties, and he said "we're up against it as neither of us has a science background." As soon as he said that, a thought occurred to me: how hard could it be to research ourselves? So I came up with a master plan: Keith and I would do as much research as we could on each of the 45 individual elements in the water. With Keith's 25 years of banking experience, he designed a spreadsheet, and we agreed that we would go through every element, find out its concentration, rarity, common uses and any health benefits.

Keith was wonderful and devised a master research plan on all the elements. The more we learnt, the more we realised there were many uses that our water could be put to. However, this was a massive undertaking, outside of our busy jobs. This water project was beginning to suck every last second of time from both our days. In fact, it became almost overpowering at times. Days rolled into nights; nights rolled into weeks and by now the last six months were almost a blur.

One day I decided to put my own energy into the water. I got Keith to print a picture of each element in our water. Then I spent a full day with these pictures, asking the angels about the healing properties of each one. It took about eight hours to go through all the elements, but the angels showed me that there were 20 with healing properties.

I asked Keith to do up a separate spreadsheet on these 20 because I felt that when I finally found a biochemist, this could help narrow it down for them. Meanwhile, Keith kept working, calling companies and universities to try and get a biochemist on board but to no avail. After many rejections, he began to think we were wasting our time. We were spending time, and money – by then we were down to the last €2,000 of Denise's original investment, and we were not getting the answers we needed.

Keith came to me when I was in my studio one day and I will never forget the look of fear in his eyes when he said "I think we need to forget about this water for a while as we are going nowhere without a biochemist." Immediately I said "no way! In fact I have such a strong feeling that I want to open up a second well. I feel that with a second well, we would be taken more seriously by potential investors." At that, Keith got angry, and told me under no circumstances were we going to open a second well, and that we had to stop everything for the moment.

We had the biggest argument in our 20-year marriage then. We really do not argue much and get on brilliantly most of the time, but that day Keith stormed out of my studio. I had a massive migraine by then and my heart was racing. There was the man I adored and he was doubting me and the water. I thought about seeking clarity from the angels about our relationship, but I knew that the best source of insight comes from within, you just need to ask for the answers you seek and then you trust those answers and yourself. I knew Keith would eventually calm down and get back supporting me and the water project.

Chapter 10

Love Conquers All

Help is at hand

After my argument with Keith I rang Denise and I said, "if he thinks I am going to forget about this water, I am not! I'll tell you Denise, I am going to open up a second well next week." Denise said the exact opposite to what I expected. She said, "Michelle, I will be straight with you, you have to respect where Keith's coming from. Now, I am coming over."

She drove straight to my studio and she sat down and said, "Michelle, do you realise what's happening here for Keith? He had a fabulous quiet life, happily married to you with two gorgeous kids, and then Tahnee lands down to you and tells you that the angels have said there are seven springs in your land with healing water. You open up this well and find there are healing properties, but you have no one to interpret the results and neither of you have a science background. Personally, I do not blame Keith for feeling like this."

Denise calmed me down, told me I needed to give Keith time and that his love for me would conquer all in the end, and said, "you need to get Jack and Dennis down to talk to him." Listening to her, I broke down crying for the first time in all the crazy months. I said "Denise I did not ask for any of this to happen to me. Am I going mad?" I told her how exhausted I was from trying to juggle family life, marriage, my interior business and get this water project off the ground. I felt a huge relief as I cried off the nine months since the angels first put me on this rollercoaster of a ride.

Denise was wonderful. She said, "Michelle, you need to chill out. Keith will be fine. Stay on track. I'm giving you another €20,000 to invest in the second well and to carry out more tests on the water." I thanked her so many times, and told her I could not get over her support of me, but I also said "I can do nothing without Keith's backing." Denise suggested I phone Jack, which I did, and told him we were all having meltdowns and that Keith did not want to continue. Jack asked me how I felt and I said, "I'm 100% convinced of the healing properties of this water, but if the man I love does not support me, where am I going?" Jack said he and Dennis would come down the next day.

The following day, they arrived, and were just brilliant. They both have a lovely way of making you feel on top gear. Dennis reassured me, and they both got the fear of the unknown out of Keith's heart.

We decided not to open the second well until we had fully researched the first, as we would only get side tracked, and Jack said a blow-out like that was bound to happen, and the air needed to be cleared.

Jack was off to India the following week and said he would call down to us again after this trip. While he was there, I sent him a few pictures of the Angel visions on my ceiling. He called me from India and said he had shown the pictures to a local spiritual man and Guruji who he knew well, and the Guruji had said, "Jack, you need to get her to India." Straight away the Guruji zoned in on the energy of me & the water and he requested that Jack bring me to India in three weeks for a week.....

When Jack came back from India he called me, as promised. He agreed that we should go to India in three weeks. I began telling Jack that my eyesight was becoming affected, that I was seeing tadpole-like shapes in my vision and that they were getting bigger. Jack said, "it's all part of the process. Just relax, feel it, and all will be ok."

That day I asked Jack to divine the second spring as Tahnee had given me another message from the angels that there was lithium in it. She said the angels had shown her that the spot was very near my studio. As soon as she said that, I felt that I knew exactly where it was.

Jack went over to the ditch to divine. Keith and Jack were chatting by the ditch and I was in the field, about 20 ft. away from Jack. The angels sent another telepathic message. They showed me a pair of divining rods that appeared in front of me, then stopped and went around the side of me, and stopped again. I said nothing and they showed me the vision again. I did not say anything, but Jack suddenly looked up at me and asked me was I alright?

I said, "the angels showed me the exact spot with a pair of divining rods. They showed me twice." Jack looked at me flabbergasted. He went on to divine and sure enough, the exact spot that Jack divined was where the angels had shown me. I really felt this was a very spiritual sign of the powers I had. I was now receiving very clear messages from my own Angels and now Jack was telling me to trust my own intuition on this journey and to have more belief in my own powers as he always felt the destiny of this water was in my hands.

A couple of days later, my parents were down having Sunday dinner with me, on a day that was cloudless and sunny; one of those perfect April afternoons. We sat outside, and the angels began showing me a vision of divining rods again, just as they had shown before. This time they showed me the same spot three times, in the middle of my kitchen window. I was trying to soak all this in while still trying to follow what my parents' were saying.

After they left, I rang Jack immediately. He told me he was doing a job in Kerry on Friday morning and would call me that afternoon. With Jack, I went to visit first my Aunty Marie, and then my parents. I introduced Jack to them, and they all loved him.

Back at home, Keith had dinner ready for us. We chatted away over the dinner and Jack said, "Michelle, your father is a healer. He has healing hands and you need to ask him can he pass down that healing power to you as you need his blessing with this water."

At this stage, no one in my family knew a thing about the water, but Jack said it was time to tell my dad that this would help me move things on. I nearly choked on my steak. I said no way, because I was worried that dad would have a heart attack.

I have always had a fabulous relationship with my father. The thought of telling him the story about the water was daunting to put it mildly. Jack's response was "Michelle, will it be you or your father that will have the heart attack?" I saw what he meant, and agreed I would tell my dad after the weekend. But on Monday morning I got cold feet, so I called Jack and I said that I felt it wasn't the right time to tell Dad. But Jack insisted. He said ring him and get him down at 12.30 and tell him the whole story. He felt I would be surprised at the way it would go.

I lit a fire in the sitting room and gave dad a cup of tea and his favourite custard cream biscuits. I was nervous and frightened of what his reaction would be. I began by saying, "I have something very important to tell you but you cannot tell anyone else, not even Mam." His first question was "are you ok? Is everything ok with Keith and the children?" I said everything is fine, and I began telling him the whole story of this journey with Kingdom Water.

When I finished, he had tears in his eyes. He said, "This is a miracle, just a miracle." He could not believe what I had done and said, "only you could do this, no one else." He told me how special I was and how all my life I had killed myself working and that God must be paying me back for this hard work. I told him about the telepathic messages from the angels and he said I totally believe you. I asked him for his healing powers and he simply said, "what do I have to do?"

I asked him to bless me, which he did with a sign of the cross on my forehead. Just like Jack, he said, "tell no one. Keep your powder dry." I have always adored my father but after what happened in my sitting room that day, I felt our bond was cemented forever. I realised how deeply my father had impacted on my femininity and my identity, and how much of an imprint the relationship with him had left with me. I felt that I needed his masculine strength and support more than ever on this journey with Kingdom Water. I felt that a huge weight was lifted off my shoulders that day.

Keith could not get the message from Tahnee about the second well out of his head and that there might be lithium in the water.

He decided to go back to Southern Scientific to test specifically for lithium in the well we had already opened. From his research, he knew that lithium is used for treating depression, anxiety, bi-polar disorder and a range of other mental health issues. At certain concentrations in drinking water, it is believed to protect against some forms of dementia.

Sure enough, Southern Scientific agreed to test again, and confirmed there was lithium in the water, 19mg per litre. I was so happy that Keith was again deeply involved in the water, and was even getting as obsessed as I was.

Chapter 11

A Trip to India

In which I meet my Guruji, Shashi

Jack has a Guruji called Shashi in India, to whom he turns to for advice, guidance, healing and spirituality. Through Jack, I knew this guruji wanted me to go to India, and Jack agreed – he felt we needed the Guruji's help with the water, because of the great power of it.

So I went with Jack. We arrived into New Delhi at 5am in the morning, and the Guruji greeted us at the airport and gave me a blessing. I was wrecked and tired. I have a bad back which was giving me trouble and had been up for 24 hours, traveling.

Even so, this Guruji got straight down to business. He is a spiritual teacher and Indian Yogi, but also a serial businessman and a world class astrologer. The energy of this man knows no bounds. He has a powerful presence, and a golden aura. And yet he is kind and unassuming, with a great sense of humour.

As we drove into New Delhi, the Guruji began to ask me how I met my husband. I told him about meeting Keith at a wedding. Halfway through my story, the Guruji stopped me and asked me what happened to my two previous boyfriends. I was gobsmacked and thinking to myself 'here I am halfway around the world in India and this Yogi is asking about my two previous boyfriends at 5am in the morning…..'

The Guruji described both of my exes to the tee. He told me that in a past life he had been my master, that I had been a princess, and Keith had been in love with me then, and that now we had connected. He began to tell me that when he first saw me at the airport, I came towards him with three old souls and that I was a very pure and genuine person. He asked me if I had any lucid dreams lately and had I ever dreamed of him. I said no. I had had several lucid dreams, but I definitely was not dreaming of him. He asked if I was sure and I said "absolutely not." Then he asked me to list all the countries I had visited in my life and I began naming them. I mentioned Australia and he said that we had worked there in a past life together.

He told me to close my eyes and asked what I saw. I said "the angels are showing me the two of us in the operating theatre together, performing open heart surgery." He told me to open my eyes and asked how did that feel?

I did not know what to make of it, except that I must have been a heart surgeon in a past life. I told him how much I loved the Rockies in Canada, and he said we had performed many open-heart surgeries in the Rockies.

He told me that I had healing hands and that I am a natural born healer and through my job as an Interior Designer I was healing people, all my life through my work. At that, I just laughed, the idea was too strange, and he told me that for the duration of my trip I was to shadow him everywhere, to get as much of his energy as possible. The Guruji spoke to me for almost three hours, and to say I was beyond tiredness at that point is an understatement.

Jack and I were staying with the Guruji, who lives in a modest two-bedroom apartment in a nice area of New Delhi. He told Jack to sleep on the floor in the sitting room and that I was to sleep in the spare room. He said that I was very lucky to be sleeping there, that a lot of saints slept in that bed.

I remember going to bed, and feeling sorry for Jack on the floor. I thought we would get a long lie in, but Jack woke me an hour later to say the Guruji was taking us to visit some temples. I remember telling Jack to get lost, that I was wrecked and my back was killing me. From the kitchen, I could hear the Guruji shouting, "Miss Michelle, get up, it is time to go and get blessings."

I knew the Guruji was testing me, physically and mentally. I quickly began to understand that this was to be no holiday. So I got up, had a quick shower and off we went in the Guruji's car to visit temples. Our first port of call was Mathura, the birthplace of Lord Krishna, where we walked along a colonnaded way in the town and then into a very large courtyard. We went into a prayer room. It was blissfully silent and peaceful in there after the hustle and bustle of the city.

Devotees circled the stone in the middle of the floor, taking it in turns to touch it. We walked up some narrow steps into the most magnificent temple, with ceiling and wall murals of Indian religious icons including Lord Krishna and Lord Vishnu.

The Guruji told me to meditate outside. As I did, a lovely warm feeling rose up inside me. Outside on the streets people were begging, and the Guruji said "feed these" which Jack and I did, with rice and vegetables from one of the food banks the Guruji has set up, to care for the poor of the city of Delhi. Young girls, the age of my Holly, were begging for food, looking weak and alone and very vulnerable. To see them was very hard. The smell of incense, of spices, the thousands of people everywhere and the poverty were overwhelming. I could not get over what I was seeing and wanted to cry and I did.

The guruji left for his office and said he would send his driver to collect us in half an hour, but Jack and I decided to walk so I could get a better feel for the city. I could not get over the dirt and dust, the insane way they drove cars. I had a headache from the tiredness and the car horns of the bustling streets of New Delhi. It was all so surreal seeing this before my very eyes.

At the office, the Guruji introduced me to all his staff and then brought us to a business meeting that lasted over three hours. Later, we went to the office of one of the men, where the angels showed me the letter T on the wall. Jack asked me if I got any feeling about the place and I explained that the angels had shown me a letter T, and that either it was a symbol for them as a team or as a three-way business partnership. I told these men they were not pulling together and they admitted that they were going through financial torment and were owed a great deal of money by a customer. I told them they needed to have more of a unified brand and before I knew it, they had me going around the building, advising them on colours and branding. By the time we got back to the apartment, it was 11pm.

The Guruji was waiting for us, with my astrology chart, and for the next two hours he went through my numbers and outlined the ways in which my future was going to change dramatically with this water. At 4am he finally told me to go to bed but said "tonight it is your turn to sleep on the floor and Jack can have the bed in the spare room." I was so pissed off! I was wrecked tired, with a bad back, and now sleeping on the floor. But I was asleep within seconds.

At 4.30am the guruji tried to wake us all up, but I let on that I did not hear him. He came over to where I was sleeping and shouted in my ear, "get up, we must visit the temples of the lost souls." I got up, but I was sleepwalking at this stage. Jack just laughed. I felt like I would be rolled over by an articulated truck, but I said nothing. I knew this was a test. In fact, the Guruji's energy alone was what got me through the next few days.

The Shrine of the Holy Souls is a very spiritual place. We walked across a courtyard with squirrels, peacocks and many other birds that began to sing in various songs. All together, they sounded like a boisterous cacophony, but I began to pick out their individual sounds and compared them with the sounds of the birds back home in my own garden.

We laid flowers that the Guruji had given us and asked the holy souls for a blessing. Afterwards, we headed back to the apartment. Although I was over 8,500 miles from my house, I had begun to feel at home in India. More and more, I felt everything was familiar. The people were so kind; they even got my sense of humour. I felt I must have a strong past life connection with India.

The Guruji said that Dr Praful was coming to the apartment to talk to me about my water, but that first I could have an hour's sleep.

I fell into bed, practically into a coma. I was so tired and it seemed I had barely closed my eyes when the guruji once again was saying, "get up....."

The Guruji, Jack and I had breakfast with Dr Praful, who introduced himself – he is a biochemist and CEO of Prashak Techno Enterprises – and said that he has patented over 200 products, has more than two decades of diverse industrial experience, primarily in the pharma industry, and has worked with, GlaxoSmithKline, Johnson and Johnson and Bilcare Ltd.

He told me he would act as my Bio Chemist consultant with the water. I showed him all my results and he tried a sample of the water that I had brought with me. I could not believe that I had travelled halfway around the world to find my biochemist and consultant, and the guy was a walking genius.

Dr Praful examined the results of the water analysis, and told me that my water had so many healing properties in it that I was looking at a multimillion-euro product. I was still speechless when we all left for the Guruji's office.

At the office, the Guruji and Dr Praful introduced me to two men. We shook hands and the men welcomed me to India. Next the Guruji said, "Michelle, I want you to explain to these men about your water." So I said, "do you mean tell them everything?" and the Guruji said, "yes, from start to finish."

I pulled out the folder that I had put together with all my notes and photos. I was overwhelmed at first, I felt strange talking to these guys about water, but I settled down and told them everything I could.

One of the men asked if he could taste the water. I handed him a bottle of Kingdom Water. I noticed the way he drank – he dropped a few drops on his tongue first, then took a few sips. He nodded his head and said the water tasted really good and he could taste the minerals in it.

I began to tell them that on opening the well, a portal had also been opened, and the water spirits had emerged. I felt strange at first, saying this, but what I had not realised was nobody in the world understands water spirits and angels like the Indians. They totally get it.

I showed the video we had made in my bedroom with the flying orbs, and neither of these men even blinked while watching it. They asked to see it a second time and then the older one said this is very powerful. The younger man said that they wanted to invest in my water and would come over to Ireland to look at the well and also to stay in my house to see the water spirits.

That meeting lasted about three hours. There was much talk about the shortage of water in India, and how I had a product to target the premium market. Dr Praful suggested that I analyse the composition of seven of the best-selling waters of the world, and compare them to mine. I thought this was ingenious – such a simple idea: buy ten top-selling brands of water and test them for the elements found in our water, and compare.

I already had a folder on all the top water brands and their labels, but this made perfect sense. I knew there and then that Dr Praful was going to be an integral part of Kingdom Water. My Guruji insisted that I go to Lourdes and Fatima and Knock, and bring back samples of the water from both places and compare them too.

The men along with my Guruji also talked about doing a massive international marketing campaign, and told me this water had the potential to be a billion dollar deal. They were specialists in water, and felt that the possibilities were huge. I had always felt, from my own research, that the water had huge health benefits, and Dr Praful agreed.

My Guruji felt that I needed to write a book about my journey with Kingdom Water. He said the book would be rolled out and that it would support the marketing campaign. I remembered what the angels, and later Patricia Quinn, had said about me writing a book, and I felt that he was right. I shook hands with all three of these men again, and they said they would see me again in a couple of months.

The Guruji, Jack and I went for lunch. As we ate, the Guruji said "Michelle I think you are unbelievable. The work you have done, the way you have explained your story, you are just unbelievable." He kept saying how lucky I was to have met Jack, and how great it was that we were all signing off the same hymn sheet.

We were chatting away and I said, "I would not be able to write a book. I'll have to get someone, a ghost-writer, to do it for me," but he said, "no, you have to write this yourself. Nobody else can do it for you." He insisted, and said that he would help me any way he could. He said I would self-publish the book and print it in India. At this, Jack, who has always had my back, said, "where do you think she is going to get the time, between her interior design business, family life and with this water project now taking up every minute? She's not a robot."

But the Guruji was adamant: "she has to write the book and she has to go to Lourdes and Fatima. I will give her a list of books she needs to read. She is a healer and, although this water will be huge, that is nothing to what is going to happen to her on an international level."

After lunch, the Guruji brought us to meet Mr Sanjeev Gupta, the CEO and chief consultant of Spice Jet, about marketing the water. He is a former CEO of Coca-Cola Asia, and has launched over 80 factories across India and Asia, as well as many water brands to give me valuable advice on the water.

That evening my Guruji took Jack and I to visit the Sai Baba Temple near Lodi road to receive blessings. It is counted amongst the most revered shrines in Delhi, the temple is quite simple from the outside but majestic inside. Sai Baba of Shirdi also known as Shirdi Sai Baba, was an Indian spiritual master who is regarded by his devotees as a Saint and a Fakir. He preached the importance of realization of the self and criticized love towards perishable things. His teachings concentrate on a moral code of love, forgiveness, helping others, charity, contentment, inner peace and devotion to God and Guruji. He stressed the importance of surrender to the true Satguru, who having trod the path to divine consciousness, will lead the disciple through the jungle of spiritual training. After visiting this powerful temple, I connected with Sai Baba & he has appeared to me many times guiding me with discovering Kingdom Water.

On the way back in the car, we rang Dennis to update him on all that was happening. He said, "Michelle, he is crazy. Where are you going to get the time to write a book and go to Lourdes, Fatima and Knock? Shashi the Guruji is having a laugh." But Jack said, "no Dennis, she has to do it." I was still trying to take it all in myself.

The following day as we prepared to leave New Delhi for the long flight home, my Guruji told me "you will be back to India in two months." I just laughed and said to myself 'is he mad in the head?

I thought to myself I will never be back here again. He told me that I had a type of energy that could hold a room, and that wherever he brought me everyone listened, and respected what I had to say. I felt I had got a massive blessing from him on my journey with Kingdom Water.

On the long plane ride home, I had plenty of time to think; about the whirlwind of a trip, everything I had learned, and the fact that I was heading back to Keith with a consultant, a biochemist and a billionaire, all interested in Kingdom Water.

Chapter 12

The Discovery of Kingdom Water –
The Manuscript

In which I decide to write a book

I was no sooner back in Ireland than Dennis phoned me to talk about what had just happened in India. He said "look you just have to write the book and put a plan of action in place." I said I would, but first, I just longed to see Keith, Luke and Holly. I was missing them so much by then.

I arrived home and sat down to dinner with my family, and I was so happy, so content. As we ate and caught up, I filled Keith in on all that had happened. I asked him to support me along the next stage as I could finally see how the last nine months were coming together. I knew that we were looking at pulling off a multi-million deal with our water, and that I had been given a serious mission from My Guruji Shashi that I had to accomplish.

After dinner I phoned Denise to tell her what had happened, and that I would have to write a book and visit Lourdes, Knock and Fatima. She laughed and asked how the hell would I write a book? But I knew she supported me fully. I said, "it's daunting to say the least." Actually, it was almost laughable – the thought of me baring my soul, writing a book, not to mention anyone wanting to read it!

That night I fell into the deepest sleep I ever had. When I woke up the angels showed me pictures of the same two men they had first showed me back in January. Finally, I recognised them – it was my Guruji Shashi and his brother-in-law, who we had also met while in India.

Later that morning, I rang my Guruji and said, "you asked me had I ever had a dream about you and I said no. But in fact, back in January, the angels showed me two men and they showed them again to me this morning. It was you, and your brother-in-law."

My guruji said again that he had been my master in a past life and that his brother-in-law had been my teacher. I asked him if this happened a lot with people he met, and he said, "very few people have your powers." I took that day off to spend time with Keith and the children. Above all else, I love to spend time with them, and I figured if I relaxed for a day, I would be rested and thinking straight, and would be able to go back into my studio and make some sort of plan of action for the future.

And indeed, the following day I came up with my master plan for the next month. I decided I had to be ruthless with my time. I booked my trip to Lourdes for three days the following week. Then I booked to go to Fatima for two days, for the Feast of Our Lady of Fatima.

I asked Keith to send the ten water samples of the top-selling international water brands to get tested with Southern Scientific, which I knew would take two weeks for results to come back.

I ordered the books my Guruji had said I should read. And then I had to tackle the backlog of interior work that I needed to do. Hours meant nothing; days were just torn off the calendar like minutes, as I moved through all I had to do.

Jack phoned me to see if I had any more thoughts on writing the book and I said, "I'm going to spend the next few days planning it out." Jack said, "stop planning and just start writing it."

And so I did. I began writing and for the next six days I did not stop. I wrote my entire journey with Kingdom Water. Keith typed it and I read the first chapters out for Denise, who thought I was on a roll with it.

I met Dennis and he read some of the book too and said, "you're flying! You're on a roll, stick with it." I felt like Tom Hanks in Forrest Gump when he started to run and could not stop. I just kept writing, remembering what my dad used to say, "paper never refused ink".

I went to Lourdes for my three-day trip. This was my third trip to Lourdes; I have always felt a strong connection, ever since our parish put on a production of Massabielle, The Story of Lourdes back in 1987, in which I played the role of Bernadette's sister. Lourdes holds a special place in my heart.

For me, Lourdes is all about the grotto and our Lady, and I spent the whole day of the first day praying at the grotto. I actually cried most of the day. I felt a release of emotions. I cleansed the baggage that I had been carrying around, possibly for most of my life. It was such a relief.

I saw water spirits & angels in the grotto and could feel their presence, and I could not help thinking of the similarities between Kingdom Water and Lourdes water.

Lourdes is situated in the foothills of the Pyrenees and Talbots Bridge is situated in the foothills of Knocknagoshel.

Bernadette was gifted Lourdes water by Our Lady, and I was gifted Kingdom Water by the angels. Most importantly, Bernadette was just an ordinary person, like me.

Prayer to Saint Bernadette

St Bernadette,

Pure and simple child,
you who were privileged to behold the beauty of Mary Immaculate
and to be the recipient of her confidence eighteen times at Lourdes;
you who did desire from then on to hide yourself in the cloister of Nevers
and there live and die as a victim of sinners, obtain for us that spirit of
purity, which will lead us also to the glorious vision of God and of Mary
in Heaven.
Amen

I went for a bath at the grotto and prayed these prayers to Our Lady for help
and guidance with Kingdom Water.

O Most Holy Virgin

Do not – in the midst of thy greatness – forget our earthly sorrows.
Cast down thy tender look upon those who suffer, who struggle against
difficulties and who cease not wetting their lips in the bitter draughts of
this life' Have pity – I beseech thee – on those who, although united in
love, have been cruelly parted, and take pity on the lonely-hearted.
Grant us thy help in our unbelief, and have compassion on those most
dear to us. Compassionate those who mourn, who pray, who tremble,
and grant all Hope and Peace.

My God, I believe, I adore, I hope and I love You!
I ask pardon of You for those who do not believe, do not adore,
do not hope and do not love You. Most Holy Trinity, Father, Son and Holy
Spirit, I adore You profoundly, and I offer You the most precious Body,
Blood, Soul and Divinity of Jesus Christ, present in all the tabernacles of
the world, in reparation for the outrages, sacrileges and indifference with

which He Himself is offended.
And, through the infinite merits of His most Sacred Heart,
and the Immaculate Heart of Mary, I beg of You the conversion
of poor sinners.

I needed to buy a suitcase to bring back bottles of water, so I walked up through the back streets for Lourdes, away from all the commercial shops and I saw a lovely old shop called Atelier Marie. The shopkeeper, Collette, had a fabulous collection of Archangel Michael's prayers and I bought some.

I got talking to Collette, and she said that she was reading a book on Saint Michael called Archangel Parle en Sicile. The author of the book had dropped her in a copy of it only yesterday.

For some reason, I began to tell her about Archangel Michael and my water. She said Archangel Michael was making this happen. She sold me a copy of the book she was reading, and told me I needed to meet the man who Archangel Michael appeared to in Italy. She said that her shop is off the beaten track, and that when a customer walks into her shop she always believes it is Our Lady who sent them. I walked away from her shop certain that this was another sign from Archangel Michael.

The Sanctuary of Our Lady of Lourdes is a very powerful place to just sit and pray, to touch the rocks under the statue or just contemplate. On my last day, I went there and asked Our Lady for guidance with the water, and made a promise that I would be back to visit her again in the future.

Two weeks later I drove to Dublin airport for my trip to Fatima.

Just a few miles from the airport, when I was on the motorway, I saw four huge 20ft angels in the sky, one with a trumpet. I took this as a sign they were watching and guiding me on my journey to Fatima, and that there was a message waiting for me there.

Then, as I drove, in the sky in front of me, I saw a vision of 50 or more rocks, with minerals dropping down from the sky. At first I thought, "my God, I could crash the car" but deep down I understood there was a strong and powerful message there.

I rang Jack from the airport and told him what had happened. He told me to text the Guruji Shashi in India, and that he would phone me when I arrived in Fatima.

I called Jack again from the bus on the way up to Fatima and he said to head straight to the main square, and phone Shashi when I got there, which I did. Shashi asked how I was and I said I felt great, at peace with myself. I could just feel the energy of Fatima within me. He told me that I needed to go and pray for an hour, and to call him back when I had done that. I prayed at the chapel of the Apparitions. I asked Our Lady of Fatima for guidance. After I phoned my Guruji and he said to pray for another hour and then phone him.

I walked up to the Basilica on the eastern side and I knelt down in front of the tomb of Francisco Marto, one of the three shepherd children to whom Our Lady appeared. I prayed the rosary. I cannot describe the feeling inside, but something told me that a miracle was about to happen. I went over to the other tombs of Lucia of Jesus and Jacinta Marto and said the rosary. I sat in the Basilica and asked all three, along with Our Lady of Fatima, for guidance on the water.

I prayed for about an hour and half and then realised I must call my Guruji Shashi. I went outside and sat down on a wall to make the call. He asked me how I was now and I said I was really at peace and something beautiful had happened to me in front of Francisco Marto's tomb. I said I was humbled to be there at the feast of Our Lady of Fatima. My Guruji then put me on to Dr Praful, who said he had been doing his own research and that we needed to trademark Kingdom Water. I told him I would do that, and that I needed to register the domain name.

Dr Praful said he wanted to devise a plan that was fair to everyone as to how the company would be divided into shares. He told me that he was looking at many different products we could use our base water for, incorporating the medicinal value, and that he was in talks with the multinationals like Coca Cola & Pepsi, and that we would be delivering a premium product to the world. I told him the water results would be back within a few days, and we agreed to talk then as Dr Praful wanted to put a final business proposal proposition to the Indian company, one that we would all be happy with. Clearly, Dr Praful meant business. I felt then that whatever prayers I had said in the Basilica, Our Lady of Fatima was helping me. That night I spoke to Jack and he said before you get the bus back to the airport in the morning go down to the square and make a promise to Our Lady of Fatima that you will be back to do the full rounds of Fatima. I said I would.

The following morning I woke at 5am and there over my bed were the angels sending me more telepathic messages. I watched this for half an hour and then realised that I had to shower and get down to the square.

Something told me that I needed to go back up to the Basilica and pray again in front of Francisco Marto's grave. It was 5.40am and still dark outside. I borrowed a bike from the hotel, for speed, and cycled down to the square and prayed in front of the chapel of Apparitions. I cycled up to the eastern side of the Basilica to Francisco Marto's tomb and kneeled down.

I said a Novena to Our Lady. As I got up, an angel whispered in my ear to kneel back down and say the Memorare prayer. So I did.

I kneeled down, closed my eyes and said the Memorare to Our Lady of Fatima:

Remember, O most gracious Virgin Mary,
that never was it known that anyone who fled to thy protection,
implored thy help, or sought thy intercession was left unaided.
Inspired with this confidence, I fly to thee, O Virgin of virgins, my Mother;
to thee do I come; before thee I stand, sinful and sorrowful.
O Mother of the Word Incarnate, despise not my petitions,
but in thy mercy hear and answer me.
Amen

I opened my eyes and there was the same angel sign on Francisco Marto's tomb that I had seen an hour earlier on the ceiling in my hotel room. I shed a silent tear and looked up to heaven and thanked Our Lady of Fatima, as I knew there was my answer. A miracle had taken place in Fatima right there before my eyes.

I promised Our Lady that I would be back to do the full rounds. I took a sample of the water from the fountain, and then I left, with the most profound feeling of relief and inner happiness. I knew that the Kingdom Water mission was about to be accomplished, thanks to Our Lady of Fatima on her feast day.

Two weeks after arriving back from Fatima, I got a calling to visit Knock shrine. I decided to go on a Sunday because every Sunday they have a rosary pilgrimage, followed by a beautiful mass. Knock Shrine is located in Co Mayo in the west of Ireland. The sanctuary of Our Lady of Knock is where an apparition of the Blessed Virgin Mary, Saint Joseph, Saint John the Evangelist, an angel and Jesus Christ (the Lamb of God) appeared on the evening of Thursday 21st August 1879.

The story of Knock is very powerful. It was about 8pm on a wet, blustery night when a local girl, Mary Byrne, from the village, was accompanying the priest's housekeeper, Mary McLoughlin, home. She stopped suddenly when she came in sight of the gable of the little church of Saint John The Baptist. There she saw standing a little out from the gable, three life-sized figures. She ran home to tell her parents and soon others from the village gathered.

Witnesses stated that they saw an apparition of Our Lady, Saint Joseph and Saint John the Evangelist. Behind them and a little to the left was a plain altar and on the altar was a cross and a lamb (a traditional Catholic image of Jesus), with adoring angels. For nearly two hours, the group of 25 people stood and gazed at the figures while rain lashed them in the darkness.

For believing Catholics, the apparition held great significance. Though it was a major Irish pilgrimage site for over 100 years, Knock really established itself as a world religious site during the last quarter of the 20th century due to the work of its long-time parish priest, Monsignor James Horan who presided over a major rebuilding of the site, including a large new Basilica alongside the old church.

Knock is famous for many cures; those who believe they are cured leave their crutches and sticks at the spot where the apparition is believed to have occurred. Many famous people, including Mother Teresa of Calcutta, have visited the site. She came in 1993. Pope John Paul II visited on September 30th 1979 to commemorate the centenary of the apparition.

On the 26th August 2018, Pope Francis visited the shrine as part of a state visit to Ireland for the 9th World Meeting of Families.

On arrival at Knock, I visited the Apparition Chapel, as this is where I feel the presence of Our Lady. The chapel was full of people. But when one lives in harmony with oneself while recognising a vital connection to the world, one can have a quiet mind, and live contentedly no matter what.

In the chapel, I prayed the Novena to Our Lady of Knock:

Give praise to the Father almighty,
To his Son, Jesus Christ, the Lord,
To the Spirit who dwells in our hearts,
Both now and forever.

I could see many orbs and angels flying behind the altar and tears began to flood my face. It is at times like this that my tears keep my soul alive in the furnace of pain. I felt I was crying for the 25 people who witnessed the apparition on that wet evening in 1879. I could feel their presence with me as I prayed. At times like this, crying seems the smartest thing to do.

It was wet outside, and as I prayed, I could see presences at the gable wall and could feel the presence of Our Lady. I must have spent four hours praying, before I began my four-hour journey back home on my own. I filled a bottle with Knock holy water as I felt I needed to bless my own site where the wells were. I remember driving home to Kerry thinking how blessed I am now to have the blessings of Lourdes, Fatima and now Knock helping me on this spiritual journey. It was like another piece of the jigsaw.

When I arrived home late that night, I lit a candle on my well and blessed the well with the water from Knock. As I did so, I looked up and I saw a massive angel guarding me over the first of the seven springs. There I was, four hours from Knock, blessing my land in Knocknagoshel with this very powerful water and asking our Lady of Knock to bless me on my journey with Kingdom Water.

Chapter 13

The Deal Clincher

In which I open all seven of the springs

Three days after I arrived back from Fatima, the water results came back from Southern Scientific. These were the analyses of the top ten selling international water brands, along with yet another analysis of our own Kingdom Water, to compare.

I spoke to Dr Praful by phone about the results, and he advised me that our water was very compatible with the very best waters out there in the international market. He also said that we had very similar healing properties in our water to the water from Lourdes, which we had also tested, and that ours was a great base water. This was further affirmation that the mineral elements were fully present in our Kingdom Water.

I had so much going on in my head at this stage. As always, there was work to be done. I needed to devise a plan with Keith and Dr Praful as to how we could go about selling this water. I also needed to come up with a sales and marketing strategy, and design a cover for my book.

I used the services of Anu Design, who specialise in book cover design.

I explained the look and feel that I wanted, and they promised they would design an amazing cover, which they did.

Minister Josepha Madigan introduced me to Enterprise Ireland, and I spoke with Nicola Nic Phaidin, manager of Food & Drinks High Potential Start-Ups. She agreed to meet with me and Keith at their head office in Dublin. She was fascinated by our business plan, but most of all by our product. We must have spent three hours with her, and she said she would come back to us with a plan that would help us, as she believed that what I needed was investment to get this off the ground.

Throughout this time, the angels continued to send me very strong messages that they wanted me to get this moving, and get the water out into the world, and to people.

I knew that Keith and I needed to have a serious talk about what exactly we both wanted from this water. We sat and thrashed out our thoughts, and we agreed that we wanted to sell the whole lot as neither of us had any interest in bottling the water ourselves. We agreed that whoever bought Kingdom Water would give us a percentage share of the water along with the sale price.

I rang a family friend, Pa Nolan, who is a serial entrepreneur, and he gave me fantastic advice. He said 'first, you need to come up with a sales pack.' So I put a plan of action in place.

I designed an 18-page brochure, outlining the story and journey of Kingdom Water, describing what was so unique about our water, along with a copy of the chemical analysis. I also designed a website and a logo, with the help of Aidan from Avalanche Design. I enlisted the services of Marek from MH Photography to take photos of my property and me, for the inside cover of the book, also a video drone of the property, as I felt that if potential buyers could see the land and product, this would be a deal clincher. I designed a folder, and planned bottle samples, so that this could all be included together in our sales pack.

The next day, Keith and I decided we needed to open the six remaining wells. We knew that if we were going to sell, we needed to know exactly what we were selling. We spoke to Denise, and straightaway she said 'I will finance this.' She said 'you need to crack on. Do not stop now, you're nearly there.'

I rang Jack and Dennis, and told them we were going to open the remaining springs. They thought this was a great idea. I booked Jack to come down and divine the six wells. He arrived, and spent the day divining the six wells with me by his side. The energy that divining takes out of your body is untold; I went to bed wrecked that night.

The following day I contacted Morgan of Lenihan's Well again, and he came up to have a look at the spots we planned to drill.

He had a look around and then he turned to me and said 'you do realise, your place is going to look like a bomb site?' I said 'sure it is only grass, it will grow back.' That night I received another strong message from the angels that the water from the well closest to the kitchen window would be different, and that we needed to be very careful when opening this well.

By now I was receiving several times a day very detailed messages and visions from my angels. I spent a lot of energy decoding these messages and conducting hours upon hours of research into the water analysis reports looking for clues and guidance on my journey.

The next day was Monday June 24th at 3.30pm, Morgan, along with his co-worker PJ, pulled into our site with their rig. I said a silent prayer and blessed all my site with the holy water from Archangel Michael's well in Ballinskelligs. I prayed that all would go well, and that we would find water in each well.

Denise called to the house and met Morgan. Instantly they hit it off. We decided to open the spring beside my design studio first. It took two hours for Morgan and PJ to set up the rig. Keith had asked our neighbour, Ritchie Walsh, for his assistance in taking away the rubble – we needed a mini digger and a dumper – and Ritchie suggested his co-worker Den Joe O'Connor from the neighbouring parish of Brosna. Den Joe had to dig up my lovely cherry trees that I planted 12 years previously. It was such an awkward spring to get at. I looked out my design studio window and saw half the garden dug up, as they had to dig a trench to carry the water once they found it, or the whole place would have been flooded. I prayed hard that all would be ok.

We hit water at 120ft and it exploded around us like a river bursting its banks. I cried when I saw the water. I could not help but think this was another miracle. I called Jack & Denise and told them we had hit a second river. They were ecstatic. That night Margaret rang and when I told her, she said 'how are you keeping your head through all of this?' I said 'Look, I have to stay focused, and therefore I do. I am on a mission and I have to accomplish it.' That night when I went to bed, the angels told me 'keep going, you cannot stop.' I saw water spirits on my bedroom ceiling that night that I had never seen before.

The following morning felt magical. I was longing for the day ahead. Dennis rang me and said "you're flying". Just stay grounded and keep going.' Then my Guruji Shashi rang me from India and gave his blessing, saying that everything would go well and that God was looking after me.

Morgan and PJ drilled the third well that day. They could not get over the flow of water – it was even stronger than the second well. They worked all day – they did not finish until 11pm – and drilled the fourth well.

Again, there was a strong flow of water, and PJ remarked that he had never seen water come out of the ground so fast and so easily. They left then, and told me they would be back the next morning to drill two more springs.

The next day, Keith and Den Joe had to prepare early, before Morgan and PJ arrived, because they needed to remove half the front section, with my lovely copper beech hedging that I had planted and watched grow over many years. They reassured me that they would reset it back once they were done.

Morgan arrived and decided to drill the fifth well in the middle of the lawn first. He told me that he would rather not drill the spot in front of the kitchen window, because it was only a foot from the path and he was afraid for the structure of the house. I said, 'Morgan, whatever you do first, you are going to drill that well after.'

He drilled the fifth well, and again found a massive flow of water. I was in my studio, and Morgan came into me and said 'there's quartz in the bedrock.' I said 'keep drilling!' The angels had told me to take a sample of the soil of the quartz from that well and test it.

Denise arrived, and she could not stop laughing. The whole site looked as though someone had dropped a bomb on it. Noel Lane from Brosna, who had helped on the very first spring we opened, passed by then, and he just looked at me, clearly wondering what the hell I was at.

Then Keith came to my studio, where I was with Denise and Noel, and he said 'Michelle, we are not drilling right in front of the house.'

I went out to Morgan and PJ then, and they asked me to ring Jack and see if we could drill six feet away from the path instead. So I rang Jack and he said 'Michelle, it's your call, but if you are going to drill that well, you have to drill where we divined the day I was with you.' I told him, 'Jack, they are all having meltdowns here.' So he said 'well, how do you feel?' I told him I would go into the sitting room alone and pray and ask the angels to give me a sign.

I did that. I went to the sitting room, prayed the Memorare to Our Lady of Lourdes, knock and Fatima, and asked Archangel Michael for guidance. Then I closed my eyes and asked the angels for help. I said 'my family home is at stake here; if you want me to drill that spot, I need a sign.' Straight away, the angels showed me a diamond coming up from the ground. I rang Jack and told him what had happened and said 'you need to pray for me now. I'm going back outside, and I'm going to get the men onsite and drill that well.'

I went out and told Keith what I had seen, and he said, 'Morgan, start drilling.' Keith believed in the power of the angels.

Morgan warned us that no insurance would cover the damage that drilling might cause, but we still said 'start drilling.' So Morgan cranked up the drill. Denise had to leave but Noel stayed to watch.

Just then, John Hegarty of Oscar Wilde Water pulled into my drive in his convertible. At that point Morgan turned to PJ and said 'this place is turning into Monaco! Denise has just left in her convertible, and that's the man who bought Tipperary Water arriving in his!' I could not stop laughing!

John had always been such a supporter of my project, and he could not get over what I had done. He is a man who believes in following your vision.

I rang Dr Praful as we were drilling, and he said 'you need to take many soil samples of this well when you hit water, and we need to test them.'

As Morgan drilled, PJ said to me 'look at all the different colours of the soil.' We could already see that this well was special and different to the others. When this sixth well was finally open, the water spurted everywhere. We were all speechless. Morgan said 'this is the most powerful well of them all.' The water did not stop gushing up. It flooded my entire driveway and even the road outside.

The stress of opening that sixth spring was unreal. I felt my heart would explode, but I knew the angels were right – this was a diamond, a precious well. I thought back to the first night that the angels began to show me telepathic signs, and how they had shown me a diamond then. I felt this was another powerful sign from God that we were on the right track.

I rang Jack and told him, and he was so relieved and delighted. Then Dennis rang me and said, 'you are unbelievable. This has gone to another level.' Tahnee rang, and she just cried with joy for me. The emotions of that day will stay in my heart forever. I shed a few silent tears myself, and I thought, here I have opened the sixth well against the odds, this is going to be massive.

The following morning, a Thursday, I walked around my property and the place was like a bombsite, but as I walked, the angels told me they were delighted with what I had done. Morgan and PJ arrived, and drilled the last of the seven springs, and again, found a massive flow of water. When he was finished, Morgan told me that never before in all their 75 years in business had Lenihan's Drilling had a domestic client drill seven wells on their property, and that surely must be one for the Guinness World Records Book!

I went into my design studio alone then, and I bawled my eyes out to think that I had done it, I had opened all seven springs. I had found seven ancient wells, all over 600 years old, and I had brought them to the light of day against all odds.

I rang Jack, and he laughed and said 'you have so much water you could keep the whole island of Ireland watered.' I rang Dr Praful and he said 'you need to come to India next week. We have to put a serious plan of action in place to sell this water.' I took samples from each of the seven springs for testing, along with soil samples, and Keith took them all to Southern Scientific.

I ordered the printing of business cards and my brochure from Walsh Print. John Hegarty had dropped in glass bottles so I could bottle my water samples. I designed labels and got them printed so that I could bring a batch of bottled samples, properly branded, out to Dr Praful the following week. The website for Kingdom Water was ready to go live.

Meantime Dr Praful had told me he had a plan of action to sell the water, but that I needed to print my book, as it would form part of the marketing and sales package. I gathered everything I needed, the entire sales package, in preparation for my trip to India.

The night before I left, Michael Murphy from Southern Scientific called to the house with the results of the water analysis. Now, every one of the seven springs has been tested, and they all show over 65 mineral elements in the water of each of the seven springs.

When I told Dr Praful the results, his response was remarkable. He said to me, "Kingdom Water is a mineral-based water, making it the most valuable natural water. Kingdom Water, with its fascinating history, has an equally functional uniqueness, having all the essential macro minerals as well as trace minerals, in the most natural form, which enables their absorption by the human system." Hearing that, I knew that I was ready to go.

Chapter 14

Angels

In Which I Describe Some Of The Angels I Met Along The Way

By the time I arrived in Delhi and met with Dr Praful, I had all the analysis reports ready. He suggested content for my brochure, and together we tweaked the website for Kingdom Water, highlighting the unique features and protecting the intellectual property of the water.

Dr Praful insisted we get a hydrologists report done on the wells – because he knew it would be very beneficial to whoever bought the water – and so I enlisted the services of Michael Murphy at Southern Scientific once again. We devised a plan to go through all the technical aspects of the water. This we did, and, in a nutshell, Kingdom Water has the potential to become the ubiquitous medium for a wide range of value-added naturally enhanced spring water formulations, which can augment the well-being, not only of those who are healthy, but also those with a range of health issues.

By now, the pain in my back, which had been steadily increasing, was very bad and my Guruji insisted I go to Aashlok Hospital to meet Dr Ashwani Chopra, a friend of his and one of the most sought-after doctors in India. Dr Chopra examined me and told me that a trapped nerve was causing the pain, and that it in turn was coming from a hernia that would need to be removed. He said I was deficient in vitamin D, and that he wanted to run a full scope of blood tests, and get an MRI and x-ray of my back. By then my Guruji had already told me that I would be having surgery, and that everything would be ok. He advised me to book in for surgery on the hernia, once I returned to Ireland. I told Dr Chopra about the water & he said that many people would want to buy Kingdom Water, and that the process would move whatever way the angels wanted it to move.

That night we went to the Shrine of the Holy Souls and fed the poor people gathered outside. This was as humbling an experience as the first time I did it. The next day I flew back to Ireland, and got straight down to work. I contacted the hospital and agreed a date in two weeks' time for my surgery. I designed the Kingdom Water brochure and sent it to Walsh Print to be printed.

My friend Denise has a great friend, Michelle Mone, a very successful businesswoman based in London. Denise wanted me to talk to Michelle, and set up a meeting in London. I brought over the sample pack and brochure I had designed, along with all the results of the chemical analysis, and we had a great meeting. I spent nearly an hour telling Michelle everything I had done. She sat and listened, and at the end said 'I think you're great, but you have to toughen up. You need to take the emotion out of this water. Whoever buys this will not care about the spiritual aspect, they will just want the water.'

She said I needed to be tough enough to look potential buyers in the eye without blinking. It was harsh, but I believe it was the wake-up call I needed.

Michelle was right, I was emotional about Kingdom Water, and that had been fine, but now I needed to be ruthless in my business dealings, just as my Guruji Shashi in India had all also advised me.

Michelle suggested that I meet her fiancé, Doug Barrowman, chairman of the Knox Group and the driving force behind this very successful group of companies. She said she would organise a half-hour meeting the following day, and that Doug would either think the story of Kingdom Water was off the walls, or he would think it was something he should invest in himself! Either way, she said, she was going to tell him that it would be the most entertaining business meeting he ever had.

Doug agreed to meet me and Denise at the Dorchester Hotel in Mayfair, London the next day at 5pm. He was, I found, kind and down to earth. I showed him the portfolio and told him my story. Once I had finished, he told me I needed to treat my business like an oil rig. He said that he was off on holidays for a month, and that on his return he would talk to Goldman Sachs about selling Kingdom Water on the open market. He said 'Michelle, you are sitting on a goldmine.' I could not believe what I was hearing. 'Goldman Sachs'….. 'goldmine…..' I was speechless and pinching myself.

Although ours was meant to be a half-hour meeting, we spent the next two hours together talking, and I gave Doug a copy of everything I had written to that point, to take away with him. He said he would read it while on holiday, and we agreed to talk again when he got back.

The day after getting back from London, I was booked in for my hernia operation, and I remember thinking great, "I'll be back to myself in a few days," I was back to working on the water project a week later when I met up with a man called John from Cahirciveen in County Kerry, Ireland, who has experience working with a couple of billionaires. At a BBQ at his house, I told John all about Kingdom Water and he said 'you are sitting on a remarkable resource with this water.'

He advised me to go to KPMG in Dublin and get advice from them before bringing the water to market. Then he said the funniest thing: 'remember that you are driving this bus and two fingers to anyone you feel is trying to shaft you in this sale, he again said do you realise that you are sitting on a remarkable resource.' That gave me huge affirmation, and I knew that he was right – that I was indeed sitting on a remarkable and valuable resource.

I rang Keith and asked him to arrange a meeting with KPMG, which he did. He and I went together, and they gave us excellent advice.

It was all action by then. I had got the hydrologist report back from Southern Scientific, and the angels were constantly sending me messages.

They kept showing me the same picture of a man in a Stetson hat I had seen in my visions.

I knew they were not showing this for no reason, and I had a strong feeling that I would meet him soon, and he would have a big part to play in the sale of Kingdom Water.

I decided to go away with Keith and the children for a few days, to Kilkenny, in southeast Ireland and then the angels sent me a message to say that the oil canvases they had told me to paint some months ago, needed to be done. There were seven canvases that were to depict different stages of my journey with discovering Kingdom Water, and I needed to paint them. I went to an art shop in Tralee to buy the materials, and while there I got a text from my Guruji Shashi, to tell me he was with me. I had never told him that my angels had told me to do this, but his angels had told him.

I had no idea what I would paint and thought about it for a long time that night. I decided to get up at 3am and see what came. I mixed together the waters from Archangel Michael's Well in Ballinskelligs and Lixnaw, St Brigid's Well in Clare, St Enda's Well in the Aran Islands, holy water from Fatima, Knock and Lourdes. I knew I wanted all these holy sacred waters in the pictures I was going to paint.

I had to paint the canvases on the ground of my studio because they were too big for any of my tables, and I painted what the angels had asked of me. They told me these paintings were sacred art, and would be exhibited in galleries around the world.

Over the last 25 years in business, I have occasionally created one-off paintings for clients who requested them for their homes or businesses, but that had always been done with a design brief in mind. This was my first time painting as an artist does – which is to express an idea or emotion in a way that elicits a personal response from each viewer. This was my artist's impression of the discovery of Kingdom Water.

Art speaks from the heart and to the heart, and I felt that what I created would contribute to spiritual wealth and development of anyone who appreciated what I had done. Once finished, I took the paintings to Tralee Framing to have the canvases professionally stretched and mounted.

A little while later, I spoke to Pa Nolan, who said that I should talk to Kevin Lane, former CEO of Ornua (a global leader in dairy products), to get his take on what I needed to do. Kevin hails from my neighbouring parish of Brosna.

He said 'you need to treat this water with all its ingredients as a separate entity.' Kevin understands ingredients – he was instrumental in bringing Kerrygold Butter to the billionaire brand it is today. He gave Keith and I fantastic advice and support, which was yet more wonderful affirmation for Kingdom Water.

About a week later, Steve Jobs, former Apple CEO, appeared to me in a vision and said that I had to visit the Neem Karoli Baba Ashram (a spiritual hermitage, monastic community, or other place of religious retreat) in Kainchi Dham in Uttarakhand state, India.

He told me that was where he got his vision for Apple. He also told me to read four books – The Seven Spiritual Laws Of Success, The Dharma Bums, The Diamond Sutra, and The Hundred Thousand Songs Of Milarepa, and that I was to bring one of these books with me to the temple. I asked 'which one?' and he said 'You will know when you receive them.'

A week or so later I was on the phone to Tahnee and she said 'there's a spirit guide trying to connect with you.' I asked her to describe what he looked like and she did so. I said 'that's Steve Jobs,' and whatsapped her, a photo of him. She said 'that's exactly him!'

He told Tahnee that he had been my spirit guide for nearly two-and-a-half years, and that he had chosen me because he felt that I think in the same kind of way that he does. I asked him again what book I should bring to the temple, and again he said I would know when they arrived. He told Tahnee to tell me to light a candle for him. That night, he appeared in my bedroom again and told me that I would get a clearer vision for Kingdom Water once I visited the temple in Kainchi Dham.

I texted my Guruji Shashi and told him what had happened, and he said 'you need to come to India and get some water energy from the Ganges, but above all else you need to visit the Himalayas and go to Badrinath, as you need a blessing for the water.' I agreed with him, and booked my flights for two weeks' time.

Before that, I decided to connect with the top six lithium experts in the world, to see if they could provide another angle on Kingdom Water. Three of the six came back to me, and one of them immediately gave me his mobile number to ring him. This was Dr Vijay Mehta who has over 45 years of research and development and manufacturing experience of ore and brine based technologies. He is the holder of 15 US technology patents. I decided to pluck up the courage to call him. He was immediately helpful and asked me to send him the chemical analyses of the water, and then to ring him in 20 minutes time. I did, and straight away he said 'I would love to help with this project.'

Dr Vijay reckoned the water could be a great source of minerals for manufacturing energy drinks. He told me that he felt very excited and confident about Kingdom Water, and would have a serious think as to how we could move forward with it. I said I would be in touch with him once I was back from my trip to India, at which stage he would be in Europe.

That same week, Keith, Denise and I went to William Fry solicitors in Dublin, who specialise in company law, and they gave us advice. I felt that we were building a strong team around us, to give us great advice around the sale of the water. My spiritual Guruji felt that all I needed at that stage was the water blessing from Mother Ganga, and the temple at Badrinath.

The day I packed for my trip to India, a parcel arrived by courier. The first of the books Steve Jobs had told me to order. It was The Hundred Thousand Songs of Milarepa. Just as he had said, I now knew which book to bring. I packed it with the rest of my things and knew that it was a sign from the angels that I was going in the right direction.

With that, I set off for India again, this time to the Himalayas.

Chapter 15

A Word About Angels

A soul is the principle of life, feeling, thought, and action in humans, regarded as a distinct entity separate from the body, and commonly held to be separable in existence from the body; the spiritual part of humans as distinct from the physical part. Basically, your soul is like a car / temple and your mind is like the engine of a car and your soul is the petrol.

Our soul body connects with angels. You do not have to invite angels into your life, because they are already with you, but for the most part, people are not connecting with them. Some people build altars in their home with statues of their favourite saints, holy pictures and place a vase of fresh flowers. Some photos of their ancestors, a selection of crystals, decks of angel cards. Clear and declutter and make room for uplifting light and energy to flow through your home.

To really connect with your angels, they require you to surrender to God, be pure in body and mind. You have to be focussed, humble and kind. The planets consolidate and energise your dreams at the most auspicious moments of your life. You need to treat your angels just like your ancestors. They need love, respect and discipline. You really need to show them care. When you are enjoying a cup of tea, make a cup for them. Place it on the altar. I always keep a glass of water on my altar for them to take a sip when they are thirsty.

Usually, you cannot see your angels. Only people who have made a connection with their angels can see them. First, you connect with invisible souls – for example, you might visit St Patrick's Cathedral, then come home and pray to him and light a candle on your altar to him. The Saint then guides the angels to you. Saints are very close to God, and angels are close to saints.

When you connect with a saint, he or she sends you an army of angels to help you. Whenever you are in difficulty, say 'Jesus, help me,' and he will send you angels to help you. Wherever they see injustice, they will help.

Angels prefer to move at night-time when it's dark as they don't like the light, but they can come any time to guide you. As God has appointed angels to live in the astral plane, they can visit you in seconds as they are running on high speed cosmic fuel. The way humans live in the human world, angels live in the spirit world. The number of angels is unlimited. They can go anywhere at any time. They are timeless and without boundaries in their travels.

The angels protect you like a mother protects her baby in the womb. Angels never die. They complete their time, reincarnate and go to God's kingdom.

The world is ruled by angels and devils but when an angel sees you living in a nice clean home with a good environment, when they see you praying and doing good deeds for friends, they want to connect with you.

They give you thousands of messages – it is up to you to work with your angels and decode the messages they send. They can do this by putting a song on your car radio, or flashing a light on and off.

Finding white feathers is an especially powerful sign. A warm sensation or a flash of light is a clear sign of angels. A tingling sensation on your skin is further validation of the presence of angels. Look to the sky and see angel clouds; these may look like an angel, or like another symbol that has meaning and significance for you. Scent is a commonly used sign from your ancestors or loved ones who have crossed over. Finding coins on your path is another sign.

When you learn to understand the signs, you will begin to pay close attention to the messages the angels are sending you. It's only then that you can understand and work with your angels in both business and spiritual balance in your life. Angels are purely sent by God to help you, love you, support you and guide you.

There are seven main archangels, arguably the closest beings to God. Archangels are incredibly powerful beings of the spiritual realm. They watch over humanity and other angels, but also over various aspects of the universe itself.

First among them is Archangel Michael, whose name translates as 'he who is like God.' He is viewed as being the lead archangel. His main role in our world is to promote courage, bravery and justice. He also protects us to keep evil spirits from leading us away from our spiritual path. I have a deep connection with Archangel Michael, firstly because I was called after him. His feast day is 29th September and my birthday is the 28th September. It was the power of visiting Archangel Michael's well in Ballinskelligs that set me on the discovery of Kingdom Water, and since being chosen by Archangel Michael for this journey, he introduced me to Michael from Southern Scientific, who tested the water for me.

As mentioned earlier when visiting Lourdes I called into an old shop where the shopkeeper had a fabulous collection of prayers to Archangel Michael, and was reading a book on Saint Michael. I told her all about the water and my journey, and she said that Archangel Michael was making all of this happen, and gave me a copy of the book she was reading. Among the angelic visions I receive about the water, the signs from Archangel Michael are the most powerful.

Archangel Michael is deeply connected to the sun and carries the energy of electrical fire, so any time you are connecting with Archangel Michael, there is the likelihood of seeing flashes of light, sparkles of light on water, blue-ish-purple orbs. These are all signs of Archangel Michael. The spiritual connection with Archangel Michael is very strong in Kerry, particularly in Ballinskelligs, part of the Dingle Diamond. Skellig Michael, a very sacred place, is at a conjunction between two very important ley lines, both of which connect with sites of great spirituality, many named after Saint Michael, including St Michael's mount, Mont St Michel and St Michael's Well.

Angels are the messengers of God. They are gifts to us from God and communicate to us from Him. They work in conjunction with your higher self and your soul's alignment. The angels don't judge your beliefs or play mind games. Instead they work with your thoughts as a way to reach you. The angels, along with your higher self, will never defy God's will.

I always trust my gut feeling. This has never let me down. I reach that state of trust with the angels in their emotional and physical feelings. God and the angels speak to us in response to our queries – we can direct a question to them and they will respond within a day or so. Sometimes you hear the answer in a song, or read it in a newspaper or see it as part of a TV advert. Keep repeating the question until you get an answer.

On this journey with Kingdom Water, the angels showed themselves to me as orbs of light. Then they began showing me telepathic messages in the shapes of rocks, and pictures of my grandmother's face. They guided me on how to open the seven springs against all the odds. Seeing angel lights is a very real and normal experience, but many people are reluctant to publicly admit this fact as they fear they will not be believed. Angel clouds are also very common – if you notice such a thing, it is another way of God letting you know that the angels are with you. This happens to me often. Sometimes they let me take photos, other times it is for my eyes only.

The angels also send signs to people to let them know they are nearby – random coins and feathers or a light flickering in your home, are signs that your angels are nearby and are saying hello. When a loved one passes, they will often send a sign in the shape of a bird such as a robin, or butterflies, or certain specific flowers that you would recognise. Anyone can receive messages from their angels. Allow yourself to be open. They will not tell you anything you cannot handle. They will not try to control your life either. Their messages help you to feel secure and happier in every aspect of your life. You can ask the angels to help you in anything, from finding a new home to helping with parenting. When you learn to start working with your angels, you will function better in your life, and it will become simpler and more peaceful.

Prayers of the Angel

My God, I believe, I adore, I hope and I love You!
I ask pardon of You for those
who do not believe, do not adore, do not hope and do not love You!
Most Holy Trinity, Father, Son and Holy Spirit,
I adore You profoundly, and I offer You
the most precious Body, Blood, Soul and Divinity of Jesus Christ, present in
all the tabernacles of the world,
in reparation for the outrages, sacrileges and indifference
with which He Himself is offended.
And, through the infinite merits of His most Sacred Heart,
and the Immaculate Heart of Mary,
I beg of You the conversion of poor sinners.

I have been chosen by the angels to bring the ancient wells to the light of day, I give gratitude by thanking them for this gift of water. As I pray I express gratitude to them. I vibrate pure positive energy throughout the universe. The angels are naturally attracted to positive energy reaching out to them from people on earth. Giving thanks to your angels will help build a two-way relationship with the hard-working angel that cares for you.

When I meditate and pray, I simply say thanks to the angels for gifting me this water and bringing this blessing into my life. Every time I see a rainbow, or a rainbow orb around the moon, or a double rainbow appears where it has not been raining, I know these are signs from my angels bringing encouragement from the heavens. Recently the angels showed me the number 7 everywhere I looked. This was another powerful sign of their guidance and wisdom. The number 7 is very powerful, and the angels have sent me this as congratulations that I am finally in tune with my true self and on the right path in my journey through the universe.

So invite angels into your life. Talk to them and listen to them, and when they respond, be grateful and thank them. Be open to their presence and help, and you too can find an angel on your shoulder. You may even find that your life is transformed, like mine on this exciting journey in the discovery of Kingdom Water.

Chapter 16

Awakenings I

In which I journey to the Himalayas

On Saturday October 8th I arrived in Delhi and met with Dr Sadhna Dixit, author of a best-selling book called "A Cure To Cancer through Naturopathy". On a first meeting with Dr Sadhna, you cannot but feel the power of her spiritual presence. She has enlightened many people and has a very strong presence that touches those who come into contact with her. Her smile is contagious and lights up the world and makes everything seem so alive.

Dr Sadhna organised my journey to the Himalayas. She found me a chauffeur, Sanjay and a minder, Maninder, to accompany me on my trip.

We set out, the three of us, at 6am on Monday 9th October from Delhi. Our first destination was seven hours away, the Neem Karoli Baba Ashram in Kainchi Dham. The Neem Karoli Baba temple is situated in the sylvan foothills of the Himalayas in Uttarakhand. Neem Karoli Baba himself was a Hindu Guruji. Outside of India, he is chiefly known as Guruji to a number of very high-profile Americans. The journey to Kainchi Dham was so breath-taking, it ended by taking us eight hours, because I wanted to stop so often to take photographs of the spectacular scenery, the people, the towns and the majestic countryside we drove through. The most characteristic features of the Himalayan mountains are their soaring heights, steep-sided jagged peaks, valleys and alpine glaciers, often of stupendous size. At every bend in the road, we took in the breath-taking pine-covered hills and fields stretching into the distance. Truly, it would fill your heart with love to just look at the beauty all around. We also passed many large farms, of rice, cotton, sugar cane, between Ghaziabad and Gajraula towns in the state of Uttar Pradesh, that contribute significantly to the agricultural economy of the region, and play a huge role in its economic growth.

The town of Ghaziabad is often referred to as 'the gateway of Uttar Pradesh' because it is so close to Delhi, and is also famous for the Hindon air force base, the biggest air power base in Asia, and the eighth biggest on the planet. Along the way, I was interested to see many small shops in every town we passed through, each serving the needs of its own community. We also passed through towns including Hapur, which has a number of old temples and has been known as one of the most important religious centres of the north. The name comes from the word 'Hapar' which means garden – a reference to the wonderful sunflowers that decorate the ditches at the sides of the road. These towns that we passed through are neither traditional in their structure, nor do they represent modern settlement. Instead, they are empowered functionally by both the city and the country. They have a unique way of life, governed by their size, site, demographic, social ecology and economy.

When we arrived at Kainchi Dham, it was almost 4pm. The temple sits at an altitude of 1400mts, and the name derives from a term used to describe the two sharp, hairpin bends on the Almora road. From the top of this road, I stopped and got out of the car to take in my surroundings, and take a few aerial photos of the temple.

The Kainchi temple is a place of special importance in the lives of every devotee who worships here. It is a place of pilgrimage, and has achieved recognition through the ashram founded here in 1962 by Neem Karoli Baba.

Neem Karoli Baba, known as Maharajji, was a great saint of the Himalayan lineage. The Maharajji was born in the village of Akbarpur around 1900 and his birth name was Lakshmi Narayan Sharma. He left his home in 1958 and became famous by the name of Neem Karoli Baba. This name was given to him by locals of the village of Neeb Karori.

He was called Maharajji by his devotees, and had a particular devotion to Hanuman, the Hindu Ape-Man like god. Maharajji's teachings were very simple and universal. Occasionally he would use the phrase 'Sub ek', meaning 'all is one'. He taught his disciples to 'love everyone, serve everyone, remember God and tell the truth.' He taught in a highly personalised, traditional way that reflected the deep devotion of the bhakti part of the heart. He was known as the 'Miracle Baba' throughout North India. He manifested many powers such as being in two places at once, or putting devotees in a state of god-consciousness at the touch of a finger.

Maharajji is best known for his unconditional love that he showered on all who came into his presence, as well as those who never met him in the body, but established a connection with him beyond the physical plane.

On the 10th September 1973 Baba Neem Karoli complained of a pain in the heart, and could no longer sleep at night due to the pain. He died at approximately 1am on 11th September 1973 in a hospital at Vrindavan, Uttar Pradesh in India after slipping into a diabetic coma. He had been returning by night train to Kainchi Dham from Agra, where he had visited a heart specialist, for the pains in his chest. He and his travelling companions had disembarked at Mathura railway station where he began convulsing. He requested to be taken to Shri Dham Vrindavan. They took him to the emergency room of the hospital. He was in a diabetic coma but his pulse was strong. He came out of the coma long enough to lift his head, pull off the oxygen mask, and ask for water from the Ganges. As there was none, they brought him regular water. He repeated 'Jaya Jagadish Hare' ('Hail to the Lord of the Universe') several times, each time at a lower pitch, until his face became serene and all his pain disappeared. He was dead.

He left no notes behind. His teachings were very simple – brief, simple stories. Usually he sat or lay on a wooden bench, wrapped in a plaid blanket with his few disciples around him. During his life, two main ashrams were built. First at Vrindavan and later at Kainchi Dham, where he spent the summer months.For him there was nothing impossible. It was at Kainchi Dham, built in 1964, that he stayed in the last decade of his life. Over the years, the temple, which is situated on the Nainital Almora road, has become an important pilgrimage for devotees from all over the world to visit.

One of the most famous stories of Neem Karoli Baba was that he once boarded a train without a ticket, and the conductor decided to halt the train and force him off at the village of Neeb Karori. After kicking Baba off the train, the conductor found the train would not start again. After several attempts, someone suggested the conductor allow Baba back on the train. Baba agreed, but only if the railway company would agree to build a station at the village of Neeb Karori. The officials agreed, and Neem Baba Karoli boarded the train again, and it immediately started. Later, a station was indeed built at Neeb Karoli.

Neem Baba Karoli was a mysterious saint who transformed the lives of many famous people, including the hippies of the 1960s, into spiritual seekers. While filming Eat, Pray, Love in India, Julia Roberts became intrigued by Hinduism. She was drawn to a picture of a holy man she had never met, Neem Baba Karoli. She found there was an instant connection.

Such was his power, he had the ability to see your past, present and future all at once, something inconceivable to most of us. His mantra to every one of his disciples was to meditate like Christ. For him to say this, he must have known how Jesus Christ meditated. He used to say "Only recite Sita- Ram Sita - Ram" and chant " Hanuman Chalisa" and "SunderKand."By reciting these you would one day become a true devotee or " Bhakta." A number of saints and enlightened masters have described Baba as "Power of Powers" or Light of Lights."

A disciple by the name of Krishna Das once asked him 'how did Jesus Christ meditate?' Baba was about to answer him, but he closed his eyes, and sat completely still. So still that it felt like the whole world had stopped breathing. After a few minutes, two tears ran down his cheeks and he opened his eyes and looked at his disciple and said 'he lost himself in love. That's how Jesus Christ meditated. He lost himself in love. He is one with all beings. He never died. No one understands. He lost himself in love.'

Steve Jobs wanted to more richly experience why we are alive, and not just make a better life. He said of his generation, so people went in search of things. The great thing that came of that time was to realise there was definitely more to life than the materialism of the late 1950s and early 60s. He was going in search of something deeper. At the time, it seemed all young seekers ended up in the same place: India.

While studying calligraphy in college, Jobs was introduced to the teachings of Neem Karoli Baba. Before long, Jobs embarked on a pilgrimage to India to meet Baba.

Unknown to Jobs, the guruji had died shortly before he arrived. Jobs visited the ashram in Kainchi Dham and made a huge connection with Baba. He spent many hours meditating in silence. Jobs shaved his head, trekked through the Himalayas and spent a month living in a one-room cement shed on a potato farm. During his wanderings, he became overcome by the widespread poverty and suffering he encountered. There is a story that the Guruji's favourite fruit was apples, and that one day, in taking a bite of one, he inspired the Apple logo. I do not know how true that story is, but I believe he was the source of much of Jobs' inspiration in creating Apple. Throughout his life, Jobs believed he had a particular connection with Baba. On his deathbed it is said that he had a picture of the guruji under his pillow. Maharaji ji once said, '' When a saint leaves his body, the temple becomes his body.''

Before things took off for Facebook, Mark Zuckerberg went to Jobs, his mentor, for advice. Jobs told him that in order to reconnect with what he believed to be the mission of Facebook, Mark should visit the Neem Baba Karoli temple, the same place Jobs went to himself early in his evolution of thinking about what he wanted for Apple and his vision of the future.

In September 2015 when Prime Minister Narender Modi of India arrived at Facebook headquarters, in Menlo Park, California, Zuckerberg told him that when he travelled in India, visiting Kainchi Dham ashram, seeing the people there and how they connected, having the opportunity to feel how much better the world could be if the world had a stronger ability to connect, reinforced for Mark the importance of what he was trying to do with Facebook. He spent two days in Kainchi Dham, meditating to Neem Baba Karoli, and, like his mentor Steve Jobs, he also began to make the connection.

Two quotes by Neem Karoli Baba that I particularly identify with are:

> *"Even if a person hurts you, give him love.*
> *The worst punishment is to throw someone out of your heart …*
> *You should love everyone as god, and love each other.*
> *If you cannot love each other, you cannot achieve your goal."*

> *"All religions are the same. They all lead to god. God is everybody. The same blood flows through us all.*
> *The arms, the legs, the heart, all are the same.*
> *See no difference. See all the same."*

Walking into the temple area, I noticed immediately how spotless the place is – this is I think the cleanest place on earth. Everything is painted brilliant white. On strict instructions from my Guruji as to how to conduct myself, I was advised 'you need to pray and meditate for an hour in the Neem Karoli Baba's bedroom, and after that meditate for another hour at the Neem Karoli Baba's statue.' I did as I had been advised.

I prayed and meditated for an hour, with the book Steve Jobs recommends bringing, The Hundred Thousand Songs of Milarepa. This, Tibetans believe, is comparable to the Mahabharata and the Bible. As I read and prayed, I heard a whisper in my ear that said 'open the book to page 43 and read.' This happened four times, with four different pages. Each time, I did as the whisper told me and read the page. On each of the four pages, the message had to do with life-changing spiritual reflection.

When I had finished praying in the bedroom, I walked over to Neem Karoli Baba's statue to meditate. This statue is so powerful. It is so life-like that at first glance, you think you are looking at a living person. I do not think I have ever seen such a beautiful statue. There is something solemn about the eyes, with an expression of serene comprehension and compassion on the face. As I looked at the statue and prayed, the angels began showing me visions – the faces of Neem Karoli Baba, my Guruji Shashi, Steve Jobs and a man with a Stetson hat. I was shown these faces several times, and I felt this was a sign, a feeling that something good was going to happen. The visions were so vivid, it was like watching a film. The visions went straight into my soul, and then I began to see the number 7 everywhere. I must have prayed there for another hour or so, when I saw a group of people arrive. It was 7pm, the time that devotees come for Aarti.

Aarti is a daily prayer ceremony offered in Hindu temples and homes, during which devotees greet and give thanks to the deities and are reminded of God's grace and glory. The word comes from the Sanskrit prefix 'aa', meaning complete, and 'rati', meaning love. Aarti also refers to a particular prayer sung in praise to the deities. After the short prayer, lighted candle wicks are passed around the congregation to allow members to receive blessings infused with the flames. Devotees often pray that their egos can be eradicated through service and humble worship, and they offer themselves in the service of God. To be part of such a prayer service was an incredible experience.

Night came early in the Himalayas, and by then dusk was falling, the mosquitoes were out in full force, and I had goose bumps on my arms from the evening chill. The white walls of the temple looked almost black. It was time to say goodbye to this sacred ashram, after a very emotional visit & having made the connection with Neem Karoli Baba. I headed back to the car and we made for our final destination that day, the Woodville Hotel, just a short drive away.

We arrived at the Woodville hotel, which has an old-fashioned Colonial charm, warm hospitality, and spectacular views of the Himalayas. This is where the Beatles stayed when they visited the area. The views were just breath-taking. When one sits in the mornings and evenings on the tops of these mountains, one can see beauty all around. If one is a spiritual person, one can understand how beauty is an inseparable part of the lord. God has to invite you to the Himalayas – he sends your invitation when you are spiritually ready.

Morning, afternoon, evening and night all have their own beauty that no language can ever describe. During the day the mountains change their colours because the sun is at the service of these mountains. In the morning they are silver grey, at midday they are golden, in the evening they are a burning shade of red, almost as if Mother Nature is dressing them to please the onlooker.

It's only when one becomes aware of the higher level of beauty which projects itself through nature, that one becomes a true artist. I realised that nature is very peaceful. She disturbs only those who disturb themselves, but she teaches wisdom to those who admire and appreciate her beauty. This is especially true of the Himalayas.

Many varieties of flower are found in abundance in these mountains. Among all the flowers that grow in the valleys, the most beautiful are the lilies and orchids. I noticed more than 25 varieties of succulents and cacti in the Himalayas, which the local people use for medicinal purposes. There are over 150 varieties of rhododendron, the most striking of which is blue and white.

I longed to pick some of the beautiful flowers, but I felt I would be depriving Mother nature. This beauty is to be admired and not used, possessed or destroyed for my own selfishness. At the top of the tall hills that surround the valley, one can see the long ranges of the Himalayas as though all the snowy peaks are tightly clinging to one another, and determined to stand from eternity to eternity.

That night I was so tired from all the travelling, I went to bed & I could not believe how much of a connection I made with Neem Karoli Baba & Steve Jobs. I felt blessed to have received their blessing on my spiritual journey with discovering Kingdom Water. It was just huge affirmation again about the spiritual aspect of Kingdom Water & I felt with Steve Jobs now acting as my spirit guide and with Baba's blessing there was no stopping me now. I fell fast asleep.

Chapter 17

Awakenings II

In which I go deeper into the Himalayas

I woke the next morning to the sound of the dawn chorus, and was reminded of the birds I once heard in the Daintree forest in Queensland, Australia. I stepped out onto the balcony of my room to appreciate the beauty of the Himalayas, the unique, rustic tranquillity and natural aura.

It is no wonder that, in Hindu mythology, the god Shiva, who resides in the Himalayas, holds a purifying power. This power is held on a personal and a universal level, and Shiva has been known to help the shedding of old habits and attachments.

We left the Woodville Hotel for our next destination, Badrinath, 13 hours away. Driving through some of the most diverse terrain in the world – along with plenty of challenging road-blocks! – it is hard to describe the feeling of Zen that came over me as I immersed myself in the nature around me.

I felt a profound sense of spiritual enlightenment, stopping often to breathe the air and take in what was around me. There were so many moments on this journey that simply took my breath away. Of all the places I have visited and travelled to, the Himalayas is undoubtedly the most spectacular.

As we were driving towards Badrinath, I felt the vibration of the Himalayas. I began to think of the great Ascended Masters, great men like Paramhansa Yogananda who wrote one of the greatest spiritual books of all time, Autobiography of a Yogi.

I was fortunate to have read this book four months before my spiritual journey to the Himalayas.

The book takes the reader on a journey into the spiritual adventures of Paramahansa Yogananda. It describes his childhood, family, the search for his Guruji Swami Sri Yukteswar Giri, to the establishment of his first school Yogoda Satsanga, to his journey to America where he lectured thousands and established the idea of self-realisation, and visited with Luther Burbank, to whom the book is dedicated.

The book then takes you on his return journey to India in 1935 where he encountered leading figures including Therese Neumann in Bavaria, the Hindu Saint Anandamayi Ma, who was Bengali and described by Sivananda Saraswati as the most perfect flower the Indian soil has produced.

Many scholars were drawn to Anandamayi Ma's light, gift, power and love, although she continued to describe herself as 'a little unlettered child'. A quote she was renowned for was

'As you love your own body,
so regard everyone as equal to your own body.
When the Supreme Experience Supervenes,
Everyone's service is revealed as one's own service.
Call it a bird, an insect, an animal, a man,
call it by any name you please,
one serves one's own self in every one of them.'

For me, chapter 33 in An Autobiography….. has to be the most powerful chapter. This is called 'Babaji, the Yogi-Christ of Modern India.'

It described the Himalayan caves near Badrinarayan, that were still blessed by the living presence of Babaji, Guruji of the great Lahiri Mahasaya, who is both ageless and eternally young. Sometimes he is formless while other times he appears before his disciples in any form he wishes, to liberate humanity from its worldly fetters.

Mahavatar Babaji remains engrossed in deep meditation in the dense forests, caves and snow-covered peaks of the Himalayas, at the same time keeping a watchful gaze on earnest seekers on their paths to the ultimate.

His divine play of appearance and disappearance, as narrated by his disciples, is his unique way of guiding his disciples on the path to divinity towards rapid liberation. He gave Yogananda the message to bring Kriya Yoga to the west, and appeared to him before his voyage.

I myself have connected with Mahavatar Babaji and have received many blessings from him on my journey with Kingdom Water. He has said: "Be it so, I shall never leave my physical body. It shall always remain visible to a small number of people on this earth."

Autobiography of a Yogi is the only book Steve Jobs had downloaded to his iPad. In an interview with the Huffington Post, Jobs called it the most important book in his life. In this book, Yogananda recorded his meetings with the great Mahatma Gandhi.

Mahatma Gandhi's mantra was 'there is enough for everyone's needs, not for everyone's greeds.' Gandhi can be looked on as one of the greatest visionaries ever born. His concepts like non-violence, and those related to truth and God, can give psychological strength and mental resilience to any individual trying to cope with the demands of life.

He considered God as 'an indefinable mysterious power that pervades everything, that makes itself felt and defies all proof.' He was an advocate for spirituality. He considered it to be a gate-keeper for mental health and he advocated for the inclusion of spirituality as a potential resource in mental health recovery and wellness.

Our first stop on the journey to Badrinath was a place called Adi Badri, a site of archaeological, religious and ecological significance Adi Badri is part of famous Panch Badri of Uttarakhand. It is a group of sixteen temples, belonging to the Gupta period. Among them is the Narayan temple, where a black stone idol of Vishnu, three feet high is enshrined. This place is within the Badri Kshetra, and Badrinath being the name for Vishnu, the temple is known as the Adi Badri.

I walked into the Narayan Temple, where a three-foot black stone idol of Lord Vishnu is enshrined, and prayed and meditated for half an hour, and received a blessing. This place is so imbued with significance and natural grandeur that ardent devotees assemble all year round to discover truth and peace, including a group of French nuns who were visiting at the same time as I happened to be there.

We set off again on our journey. However, the road from Adi Badri to Badrinath is highly dangerous, narrow and winding. Traffic is controlled by allowing vehicles to travel in only batches, at a speed of 20km an hour.

I could not help but think of the great Himalayan Master, Swami Rama, who had received his spiritual training in the Himalayan cave monasteries. He roamed the Himalayas for more than four decades and was educated by their great sages. He considered the Himalayas as his spiritual parents, and living there was like living in the lap of a mother. In addition to his intense spiritual training, Swami Rama received higher education in both India & Europe. In 1969 he went to America where he founded the Himalayan Institute. While driving along I could almost feel his presence in the Himalayas.

Rains can easily disrupt the flow of traffic, and there had been recent rainfall and landslides. Along the route is the city of Joshimath, a sacred town that spreads its aura across the entire region. It has a temple dedicated to Narashima, an incarnation of Lord Vishnu, and is home to two mighty rivers, the Dhauliganga and the Alaknanda, which meet at Vishnuprayag, overlooking the town. The road from Joshimath to Badrinath is at a height of 6150 ft, and is known as the gateway to several mountain climbing expeditions, the King trails and pilgrim centres. Watching the scenery unfold from the car window, seeing the Himalayan mountain peaks is a profoundly awe-inspiring sight. I realised that this is truly God's country.

About 20km from Badrinath, we found the road before us blocked by a mass of rock and debris from a landslide. Maninder, my guide, said we would have to walk the rest of the way. So we packed a light overnight bag each, and set off. We passed tourist buses and cars, also abandoned on the narrow road where many before us had chosen to walk, with no phone signal and nothing to guide them except the local knowledge of rivers and pathways.

I was ecstatic to be hiking through the mountains. The fresh clean air going deep into my lungs gave me such a burst of energy that I felt I could walk for miles. Anyone would find such a walk through the mightiest mountain range on earth fascinating, perhaps daunting, but for me, it was the most spiritually exciting, wildly adventurous, intensely beautiful and serene place I have ever been. What I had not previously realised is that you do not have to be an athlete to walk through the Himalayas – that the energy and pure spirituality of the place will get you through.

We eventually arrived into Badrinath, and I felt that I understood the feelings of Pope John Paul when he came to Ireland, and bent down and kissed the ground. Getting there had been a triumph over pitfalls and adversity of various kinds, but once in the holy town, I knew how right it was for me to be there.

Badrinath is a town of just over 840 people, elevated at 10,170 ft, on the banks of the Alaknanda river, and is one of the most-visited pilgrimage sites in India. The people of Badrinath Mana village do not suffer from materialistic insanity. The villagers are dependent on the plains only for salt and oil to burn in their lamps. Life here is calm and peaceful. These people do not know how to hate anyone. These people led simple lives close to nature. The life span of the people is often over 100 years. The town was established by Adi Shankara in the 19th century, but even before that, pilgrims would walk hundreds of miles to pray here. This is one of the four sites of India's Char Dham pilgrimage, and the town is named for the temple of Badrinath ('Badri' refers to a berry that grows abundantly in the area, and also means 'Lord'), the most powerful of all the Vishnu temples, where, the legend goes, Lord Vishnu completed 1000 years of meditation under a Badri tree, for the good of humanity.

This is the only temple I know of where men and women perform rituals and prayers for six months of the year, and where the angels take over for the next six months, as the place becomes inaccessible through the winter due to harsh weather. Elderly spiritualists who visited would often find that their final journey from this life began in the six months after their sojourn here, perhaps because there is a direct path to heaven from the temple.

I had been advised to go to the hotel we had booked and leave our bags, then head to the temple, to pray and meditate for two hours. I did so. The temple is about 50ft high, with a small cupola covered with a gold roof on top.

The architecture is reminiscent of a Buddhist temple, with a brightly painted façade, and has gone through several major renovations due to its age, and the damage caused by avalanches.

As per instructions I took a bath in the natural sulphur springs before I went into the temple. The sulphuric water is believed to possess medicinal properties, particularly for skin diseases, and devotees will usually bathe here before entering the temple – in a process known as 'Agni Teerth,' which is believed to wash away sins and purify the soul.

On entering the temple, I could not get over the beauty. Inside, it is so huge, that I felt it was the Las Vegas of temples, with all its bright lights flashing. One legend has it that when the goddess Ganga was sent to earth to help humanity's suffering, the earth was unable to withstand the force of her descent, and the mighty Ganges was split into 12 holy channels, with the Alaknanda as one of them.

I sat and meditated for an hour and asked a blessing of the local saint venerated in the temple. Outside, the market was in full flow. Because this is a highly revered pilgrimage destination, the artefacts on sale were mainly religious. There were a multitude of small shops around the Badrinath temple selling trinkets and souvenirs; one of the most sought-after being a miniature representation of the sacred shrine of Vishnu, who is the main deity of the temple.

At this stage, I was exhausted, and we went to our hotel for dinner, then bed. Night fell fast on the town of Badrinath. No more than an hour earlier, the sky had been painted with hues of red, orange and pink but now all colour had faded, leaving only a matt black canvas with no stars to be looked upon. Luckily I had been warned about the cold, although nothing can really prepare you. I slept that night wearing my insulated North Face jackets & under armour and leggings, a wool hat and two duvets, and I was still freezing. I will never forget the cold. It is the type that reaches deep into my bones, as if my heart were a door left open to the icy wind.

I woke at 5.30am the next morning for breakfast. Our first port of call was to walk the 3km to the Mana village, the last Indian village before the border with Tibet and China. It has been designated as a specific 'tourism village' by the Uttarakhand government. The village is on the banks of the river Saraswati (Saraswati, also known as Sarasvati, is the Hindu goddess of learning, wisdom, music, and aesthetics), and the people who live in the area are known as Bhotiya (ethno-linguistically related Tibetan people). The villagers of Mana live in small cottages that are gracefully decorated and carved. Each resident has their own plot of land and grows the most amazing potatoes, cabbage and vegetables, as well as knitting wonderful woollen garments.

As an outsider looking at this village, you would be forgiven for saying these people have very little, but I believe they have all they need. Their lives are simple. They eat the best food – we might call the produce organic, for them it is just their natural fare – breathe the best air in the world into their lungs, and live in the most spiritual place.

I met several old men and women of the village and chatted with them in their humble homes. To me they were the real heart and soul of India. Kind, helpful, decent spiritual people with large hearts. I felt really at home here & felt a real past life connection with the place.

Traces of Hindu mythology – Mahabharata – are visible in Mana, and it is believed that the Pandavas (the five sons of Pandu, a king of the Kuru dynasty) passed through here on their journey to heaven. There is a famous stone bridge, created out of a huge rock, apparently by Bheem, one of the five brothers, over what is known as Bheem Pool near the Saraswati river. At the end of the village, standing proudly, is the last tea shop of India, where I enjoyed a nice cup of tea.

I visited the Saraswati Temple next to the Saraswati river. The river is visible above the surface for 100 metres at this point, before it submerges underground and travels a distance, to finally join the confluence of the rivers Ganga, Yamunanda and Saraswati at Sangam near Allahabad. Numerous sages such as Narada, Bhrigu, Vashishta, Lord Krishna and others have meditated and attained salvation along the banks of this holy river.

As I left Mana, I visited the Viyasa cave and received a blessing. I bought some scarves hand-knitted by the women of the village, because they are beautiful, and to support their livelihood.

As we left Badrinath, I felt I had reached the summit of my trip. I felt a huge connection with the place. As I poured some of the Kingdom Water I had brought with me into the Saraswati river, I knew that Badrinath would always have a special place in my heart, as part of my journey of discovery. And indeed, memories of these experiences awaken me even today and I feel the Himalayan mountains are calling me back.

Maninder and I headed back, traveling down the Himalayas to return to our car and drive the 12 hours to visit Devprayag, home of the Ganges river. As we trekked back through the mountains, I could not help but feel that this journey, and visiting so many different holy places, had strengthened my spirituality and recharged my energy with all the blessings and protection I had received along the way. These places are widely known for their power and cosmic energy. Many Yogis, Sages, rulers and others aspire to visit these places at least once in a lifetime, and here I was, achieving this.

During our hike, I saw a vision of a man wearing a big black cloak with a hood. He looked like a monk and carried a stick. I felt this was another sign from the angels that they were guiding and minding me on my spiritual journey through the Himalayas.

I am a pretty fast walker, and was ahead of Maninder by about 2 km when a soldier blew a whistle close to where I walked with a group of others I had encountered along the way. The soldier stopped all those of us walking. He spoke to me in a language I did not understand, then pointed up to a landslide that had occurred. Further up the side of the mountain, at a shear angle, there was another man directing a digger that was removing rocks from the path, and sending some falling further down the mountain as he did so. It seemed like a suicidal undertaking for any workman, to put himself in such danger to clear a landslide.

As I looked, the ground under the digger began to move and slide further. The soldier blew his whistle fast, signalling us all to run. So I ran. As I did so, I looked back and saw the poor man directing the digger fall thousands of feet, to his death. I cried and cried as I ran. There was nothing anyone could do for him. I thought about the man, and how he was some woman's son. I thought about my own children, and I froze inside. I must have run all the way back to where we had abandoned our car, and then could run no more. I sat on a rock, and I cried. A man who had witnessed everything came over to me and simply shook his head. There was nothing anyone could say.

There are moments like this in life, where we witness something that makes us stop and think, and realise how lucky and blessed our lives are. That moment, seeing that man fall thousands of feet to his death, will haunt me forever.

Chapter 18

Awakenings III
The Mighty Ganges

When Maninder arrived back to the car, we set out again on our journey to Devprayag. I had been advised we must visit the temple of Dhari Devi, located on the banks of the Alaknanda river, in the Garhwal Region of Uttarakhand state. The temple is home to the upper half of the idol of the goddess Dhari, while the lower half of the idol is located in Kalimath, where she is worshipped as a manifestation of the Goddess Kali. Dhari is considered to be the guardian deity of Uttarakhand and is revered as the protector of the four Char Dham pilgrimage sites. Her shrine is one of 108 Shakti Peetha in India, as numbered by Shrimad Devi Bhagwat.

The village near the temple is named for the goddess, and known as Dhari village. On 16th June 2013, the original temple of the goddess was demolished, to make way for construction of a huge hydro-electric dam. Hours after the idol was moved, the region suffered what is one of the country's worst natural disasters, after the 2004 tsunami. These were the 2013 North India floods, otherwise known as the 'Himalayan Tsunami', and were caused by a multi-day cloudburst, resulting in devastating floods, and landslides that washed away the entire shrine and the town, killing hundreds of people and leaving the hydroelectric project in ruins. Fortunately, although the Shrine was destroyed, the statue of Dhari Devi had been removed that morning and taken to a concrete platform high above the river so that it was not submerged in the flash floods.

Many locals and devotees believe that Uttarakhand had to face the goddess as she was shifted from her original abode.

The new temple is now being constructed on the original location. Approaching it, I crossed the river bridge and noticed thousands of bells hanging from each side of the bridge. Monkeys gathered all around the bridge, setting the bells tinkling gaily in the bright air. On entering the temple, I met with a local man who sat me down and asked where I was from and who I was. He began telling me that Dhari Devi changes in appearance throughout the day, from a young girl in the morning, to a woman in the afternoon, and finally an old lady in the evening. He told me that I must ask the goddess what I wanted, and that if I received it, I would have to come back and visit the temple again and leave a present of a bell. He said 'did you see all the bells hanging on the bridge and around the temple? These are the reminders of blessings that have been granted to people all over the world who have prayed to the goddess.'

The temple has a divine feeling and I was very conscious of the power of the goddess. The view around the temple is enchanting, with high green mountains.

I sank down in front of the goddess and asked her to help me get Kingdom Water sold and released into the world to help people just as the angels had wanted. While praying, I noticed a face on the rocks behind the goddess' head, and I also noticed that the rocks changed colour, turning gold.

As I sat there praying, my legs began to shake. I had no control over them and could not stop them trembling. Eventually after I got up, I went back over to the local man and told him what had happened. He told me that I had spiritually connected with the goddess and that I had to promise to come back and visit again, with a bell. I said I would and I left the temple and crossed back over the bridge, looking at all the many, many bells that decorated it. The sight sent a small spiritual shiver up my spine. Since that day Goddess Kali has appeared to me on numerous occasions when she felt that I needed her powerful energy to guide me on my spiritual path.

As we drove away from the temple, it was impossible not to feel the devastation caused by the floods and landslides and see the damage that was still evident. I felt a strong connection with Dhari Devi, a place built on water, because of my own journey with Kingdom Water.

We drove the remaining distance to Devprayag. On arriving at the town, I stopped and got out and took several more photos of the spectacular scenery again my whole body started to vibrate, I began to cry. The feeling was almost overbearing at times and I could not understand why I was feeling like this. But the moment I set foot on the path down to the Ganges, I felt emotional. It was as though I could feel the sacred river run through my entire body.

Hinduism is the world's oldest religion and to quote from the Mahabharata:

> *'Verily, Ganga is the path to heaven of those that have bathed in her current.'*

Walking across the suspension bridge, over the Ganges, was something special. I stood still for a moment to try and take in my surroundings. Around me, little riverbank shops were selling everything from plastic souvenirs to Smeg fridges.

I reached the river itself and followed the instructions given to me by my Guruji: 'just sit and pray and be sure to bathe in the water and pray to Holy Ganga with the following prayer:

"Holy Mother, please, Mother, I am so grateful to you for giving me the chance to visit you. I myself and my near and dear, and my ancestors, those not in physical form, on behalf of them I am praying to you. Please accept my prayer."'

I was told to be very careful near the riverside as the current is fast, and there are many angels present.

I said the prayer my Guruji had told me. I had brought a small bottle of Kingdom Water with me, and I poured it into the Ganges and got the blessings of the Ganges. This brought a wonderfully liberating and spiritual feeling. It was so powerful to know that Kingdom Water was now flowing through the Ganges. I sat down on a step and prayed.

As I did so, a voice inside my head said, "Look at the water." When I did, I saw many angels.

Then, as it began to get dark, in the distance a light flickered on and off and a voice in my head said 'keep watching.' With that, an angel some 20ft high appeared, flapping her wings. I went to take a photo, but the photo came out blank. Then Our Lady appeared to me, with Saint Martin, Saint Padre Pio, Neem Baba Karoli, along with my Guruji and Steve Jobs. I could not believe what I was seeing. Then I saw the same man in the Stetson hat I had seen before. The faces flashed three times. Then I saw my grandmother, Mary Bridget, and finally Our Lord, on a crucifix. It was utterly overwhelming and emotional; a million different emotions wrapped into one.

Along came a young boy, and gave me a bowl of food to feed the fish, which I did. I was given a blessing from one of the priests known as 'Pandas'.

Because of the purifying nature of the river, Hindus believe that any rituals performed at the banks of the Ganges will bring fortune and wash away impurity. There are seven sacred rivers in India, of which the holiest is the Ganges. The waters of the Ganges originate in the frozen heart of the Himalayas. The river travels thousands of miles across the plains before flowing east into Bangladesh and from there spilling into the Bay of Bengal. Mother Ganga is described by ancient Hindu scriptures as a gift from the Gods – the earthly incarnation of the deity Ganga. It is, above all, the river of India, and has held India's heart captive and drawn uncounted millions to her banks since the dawn of history.

For thousands of years the Ganges has been held sacred and is repeatedly invoked in sacred Hindu texts including Vedas, Mahabharat and Ramayana. The river Ganga is not just a river, it is an all-giving and all-forgiving Mother.

The Hindus call it 'Ganga Maiyya' with love and devotion. The river takes on the form of a sacred goddess who absolves all the sins gathered in a lifetime. Mother Ganga talks everyone into her loving embrace after death.

So holy is the water that people travel to her shores to bless the remains of their loved ones in it. Her waters are considered so pure and so powerful that when immersed in it, a person is washed of all sins and becomes eligible for entry to heaven by the simple act of pouring a handful of water over one's head and letting it run down over the body.

Moving, flowing or falling, water is believed to have great cleansing powers. Water absorbs pollution, but when it is flowing, like a river, it carries pollution away. The word Ganga is derived from 'Gan' meaning 'to go' and indeed, Ganga is the swift-goer and the energetic movement of the water is constantly mentioned as one reason for her purifying attributes. Ganga's fall from heaven is replicated daily in thousands of Hindu temples where water from the Ganges river is poured over the sacred Shiva Linga.

Ganga water is used in all Hindu prayers and ceremonies. Before someone dies, Ganga water is placed in their mouths. Just as in Ireland holy water is used to bless people and homes, in India Ganga water is used to purify a house and those who wash in it.

Hindus view the Ganges as a birthplace of the divine, and the river is believed to be a crack in the physical world where the supernatural can slip through and immerse us mortals in its wonders. Ganga water is also used for medicinal purposes as it contains many minerals and passes through many plants and herbs. Most people who come to the Gages do so because they have a spiritual thirst they want to quench. quite simple, the river Ganges is the river of heaven.

I decided to bathe in the water, observing the Ganga Aarti devotional ritual as I did so. This is a unique experience. Being at the side of the Holy River is a once in a lifetime experience.

As I bathed, I marvelled at the fact that the water was much cleaner than I had expected. Bathing there was a raw, intense feeling. Such an experience will leave a mark on your soul and change how you think about life. It will stay with me forever. As I grasped the rope that is placed to help bathers out of the water, the figure 7 appeared on the pillar next to my left hand, and I was able to take a photo of it. I was also lucky enough to get a few beautiful photos of some angels that appeared to me in the sky.

I filled two bottles of water to bring home to bless my seven springs with. As I left the Ganges, I noticed a gorgeous hotel called the Ramkund Resort that has the best location and the best views – the perfect place for anyone wanting to stay and wake up to breath-taking views over the river.

I had spent nearly three hours there. We were heading back to Delhi that night by car, and I left the Ganges with a heavy heart. It was night-time and the roads were quiet. We passed through much rough terrain. We passed towns including Rishikesh, home to the most difficult and exhilarating white water rafting. It's in the foothills of the Himalayas, and I decided that on any future visit, this would certainly be on my bucket list.

It began to rain as we drove and for a moment, looking out the window, I felt I was back home and not 8500 miles from Knocknagoshel.

It was 4am before we reached Delhi. To say I was tired is an understatement. I slept for a few hours and then got up and packed properly as I was heading home the following day. I spoke to my Guruji Shashi and described my trip in detail. He could not get over how much I had seen and done on such a tight schedule. I had achieved a spiritual journey through the Himalayas almost entirely on my own. No phones, no internet, no online presence. Electricity and running water became luxuries and the time alone was more intense than I expected. I cannot say enough about the wonderful, powerful experiences I went through.

The amazing people I met on my pilgrimage and the huge connection I had made to the great ascended Masters. To feel the amazing power of so many sacred places and people was remarkable.

It was a divine experience for me. Not everyone feels the same. Not everyone will get it – in fact, nature will not allow some people to get it, or even to go there – but I did. For anyone who doesn't like to travel alone, there are tours to join. They do great package deals and they will arrange everything and tailor-make a trip that suits your needs.

While driving through the Himalayas, I asked myself many times, if India is spiritual, then why is there so much poverty? I now realise that these are two entirely different things. Religion and politics have always remained separate in India and spiritual people do not become involved in politics, but now when I hear President Modi speak, I feel for the first time a president with a spiritual voice inside him. Maybe that will be a game-changer in dealing with so much poverty in the country. Throughout this journey I'm on, and knowing all these great Masters and Saints, along with my own ancestors, are guiding the path of destiny with Kingdom Water, I feel so privileged, humble and blessed.

That journey through the Himalayas will last in my soul and my heart forever. I cannot overestimate how much this trip has contributed to my spiritual journey with Kingdom Water.

If anyone ever asks me why India, my response will be simple:

Go there. See for yourself. Life does not need to be changed; only our attitudes do, this is the real secret.

Now, I look back now on my journey and all I can do is cry to think of what I have achieved, against the odds. No matter who buys this water, it is going to have an effect on so many people's lives. I do not think it has fully sunk in yet. Someday I'm sure it will. I could not have done this without Keith, and the support of My Guruji, Denise, Tahnee, Dennis, Jack, Dr Praful, my dad and my family, but most of all, I could not have done this without the deep faith I hold in my heart.

On this journey I have realised many things, powers in myself that at first I could have never imagined. I have the ability now to see the happenings of the future. God only gives this wisdom and knowledge to very few people. The only person that can experience what I have achieved to date, has to have had a kundalini awakening. When a kundalini awakens in a person, the chakras awake. Only then can you see the future and connect with God and attain self knowledge. The most important thing for a human being is to attain self knowledge. This is my story, a hauntingly beautiful and deeply inspiring journey of a kundalini awakening within Michelle Keane.

This journey has asked so much of me. My energy, spirit, health and wellbeing all have been challenged by the things I have been through since the day I first visited St. Michaels Well in Ballinskelligs and heard the messages I received from my Ancestors. There have been many times along this journey that I have been utterly exhausted and depleted, but one thing for sure is that throughout this journey I have never stopped believing in the power of this water that has come to me so unexpectedly, and the power of Mother Nature. At times I may have doubted myself but I never doubted the power of Kingdom Water.

The World has awakened now to water trading & the value of Water. According to a Bloomberg report issued on Friday 18th September 2020, Wall Street is about to start trading future contracts on the state's water supply. Markets are known to be future looking and that is exactly, it is doing by introducing water as the new trading commodity. They are now realising that almost two – thirds of the world's population is expected to face water shortages by 2025, according to the CME. Tim McCourt, the global head of equity index and alternative investment products at CME, said in an interview " that water scarcity is certainly one of the biggest challenges facing communities and individuals today across the globe, where currently about 2 billion people are already living in countries experiencing high water stress".

Governments, businesses, universities and citizens around the world, are waking up to the water challenges, and beginning to take action.

I cannot help but think back to when my Aunty Brid was dying, 30 years ago, when I was just 15. She whispered in my ear that she would never forget what I had done for her, and that she would always look after me. Well, she has looked after me. She is my guardian angel, and I am perfectly sure she is having a good old laugh up there in heaven now.

What happens next is in the hands of God and the angels. But I know that my mission with the seven springs is complete.

I have released the water, as the angels wanted and directed me to do, and now I wait, knowing that my bit is done, for the next stage to begin.

I believe this water will reach many people, and will bless many lives. I am honoured to have been a part of that, and I look forward to the next stage of this miraculous journey of KINGDOM WATER.

Acknowledgements

My angels I met along the journey.

There have been countless people who have come into my life at times when I greatly needed them. I now realise that these were angels sent by God to encourage and strengthen me on my journey. I am so fortunate to have been blessed in life by incredible friends and family, colleagues, mentors. This book wouldn't exist without them.

I want to thank my closest family. My own little Brady Bunch! I am so blessed and grateful to my beloved husband Keith of 20 years, my soulmate and twin flame, my rock and the absolute love of my life, who to me is the real hero in this book. I could not have written this book without his support and encouragement on my spiritual journey. I am so grateful for the most amazing son, Luke, a true old soul that he brought into my life. And to my Princess Holly, my beautiful daughter, you are the four angels in heaven all wrapped up in one. Both births blessed me more than either of you could ever know. Thanks for being the best son and daughter a mother could ask for.

A sincere massive thank you to my Indian guruji, Shashi, for believing my story and encouraging me to write this book. He came alongside at just the right time to help me see what this book could be, helped me get the stories out of my heart and onto paper. His tireless dedication to the process has helped this book emerge into the spiritual treasure it is.

Also, gone but never forgotten, are my beloved Noelle, my four angels in heaven, my beloved Auntie Brid (my guardian angel), my beloved Auntie Kathleen (my spirit guide), my beloved grandparents Michael and Mary Bridget Cullinane, and Maurice and Nora Mary Keane (my spirit guides), my beloved classmate and friend Ella McAuliffe (angel).

Special thanks goes to my mother, Therese and my father Luke, for bringing me into this world and for giving me this beautiful gift of life. Also to my sisters Norma, Myra, Delia and my brother Maurice for all their support throughout my life.

A special thanks to my mother-in-law, Goretti and my father-in-law, William for giving me their son Keith, the best husband and father a wife could ask for.

Thank you to my friend Tahnee for bringing this dream and vision into my life. A special thanks to Denise my dearest friend, for simply believing in me and for putting her money into backing my journey with Kingdom Water. To Jack, for enriching my life by teaching me so many spiritual ways. I want to thank him for divining my land.

Thank you to Morgan Lenihan of Lenihan's Drilling for drilling the wells for Kingdom Water. A special thank you to Jack Curtin, known locally as 'the Water Doctor', for supplying and installing the pumping system, and to his partner in crime, Mike Donaghue and my brother Maurice for all the groundworks. A special thank you to Michael Murphy of Southern Scientific for Testing all the Water Samples. To Dr. Praful for his expertise, his words of wisdom, kindness and guidance throughout this journey with Kingdom Water.

I'm so grateful for the special friends, neighbours and relations who have graced my path. I thank my girlfriends close to home and overseas, who I can count on no matter what, my true angels that I met along the way. There are way too many to mention here but you know who you are. For all your love and support throughout my life I say a sincere thank you to one & all.

Finally I want to say thank you to God, Our Lady, Mother Nature, My Ancestors and all the Saints, Ascended Masters & Spirit guides that guided me on discovering Kingdom Water against all odds, and for never asking me to do anything I was not equipped to do. It is only true your grace and Divine Mercy, that I have made it this far. Namaste & Amen.

"Arise Knocknagoshel and Take your place among the nations of the earth"

Charles Stuart Parnell – 1891

Praise for Kingdom Water

Author Michelle Keane guides us on a remarkable spiritual journey through discovering Kingdom Water. Since humans and the earth are composed mostly by water, her message is very simple that science and spirit are united, it is only through them, that we can only view the entire universe and reclaim our health and create peace.

This Spiritual treasure confirms our deep and lasting connection to water – our most precious resource. Water is to the body as oil is to the car, the more water you drink the more you run!

Pure water is the world's first and foremost medicine. It needs no doctors prescription, it is freely available & it costs nothing.

We must treat water as if it were the most precious thing in the world, the most valuable natural resource.

Dr. Ashwani Chopra,
M.B.B.S. M.D. (DELHI) M.R.C.P. (LONDON),
Consultant Physician Gastroenterologist,
Director AASHLOK Hospital,
New Delhi,
India.

Please Review

Dear Reader,

If you enjoyed reading this book, would you kindly post a short review on Amazon, Goodreads or what ever platform you purchased the book from? Your feedback will make all the difference in spreading the word about my book. It would mean so much to me also as most potential readers do judge a book by what others have to say. Thank you in advance for your kindness.